Basic Churches are Real Churches:

Biblical Support for Simple Churches, Organic Churches, House Churches and Congregations That Grow Out Of Church Multiplication Movements

Ebbie C. Smith

Church Starting Network

Unless otherwise noted, Scripture quotations are from the Holy Bible, New International Version © 1973, 1978, 1984.

Library of Congress Cataloging-in-Publication Data

Ebbie C. Smith

Basic Churches are Real Churches: *Biblical Support for Simple Churches, Organic Churches, House Churches and Congregations That Grow Out Of Church Multiplication Movements*

ISBN 978-0-9820875-8-9
0-9820875-8-6

1. Church Growth 2. Basic church, house church, simple church,

Contents

Chapter

Pre Word

Note that this section is called "Pre Word" not Preface. These paragraphs will be a little different from the usual preliminary words. These ideas are intended only to establish the playing field and help you understand what I am trying to say.

One would have to have his or her ears shut not to hear multiple voices speaking about simple churches, house churches, basic churches, cell churches, multi-housing churches, and other expressions of gathered Christianity. How should the Christian movement respond to these voices?

This book will not suggest that these new expressions of Christian congregations compose the one and only expression of Christian fellowship and ministry. Neither will you hear any proclamation of the death and burial of the "Traditional Church." This book is only a plea that simple churches, basic churches, house churches and the like be accepted a valid and proper expression of Christian fellowships.

Equally heard in today's world are calls for employing the methods that lead to what is being named, church-planting movements. These movements are rapid and expotential growth of congregations among a particular people group. This book will not hint at the idea that this way of evangelizing is the one and only method. This book simply begs that these movements be accepted and recognized as valid, acceptable, and important movements of God's Spirit.

Too often people reject newer methods because those who develop the new ways seem to suggest or even teach that the old is to be tossed aside and the new become the standard. This idea often clouds the efficiency that still resides in the old and covers some areas of lack in the new. A wiser course seems to be to affirm both the older means and the newer. The Spirit of God uses many ways to achieve the plans of God.

Look with us then at these ways of proclaiming the Word of God and gathering the people of God and achieving the will of God. Basic churches (as we will call them) and Church Multiplication Movements (as we will name them) are valid, acceptable, productive means and God's servants who seek to use them should be allowed, respected, encouraged, and freed to employ these means to seek His goals.

These pages are penned with the prayer that God's people will learn to strive together to reach His purposes. Let learn to encourage rather than restrict. Let us learn to empower rather than control. Let us learn to sing in concert rather than in solo. Let us learn to join hands rather than shake fists.

The writer of Proverbs promotes the truth of the advantages of working in concert. A single locust has little power. When the locusts advance in great numbers, however, they cause widespread destruction (30:27).

The Christian movement will find great power in mutual encouragement and joint action. This book seeks nothing more than this.

CHAPTER 1

WHAT IT TAKES TO BE A CHURCH

Henry and Martha finish the last minute arrangements to their living room and begin to greet their friends who are coming for worship and Bible study. Soon five couples and one single man sit in the room with open Bibles. Twelve children also hear Bible stories in the basement family room where several teen-aged young people care for the smaller offspring. The group believes fervently and accepts fully that they form a segment of the *Body of Christ*.

Henry opens with a prayer, a request for two lost persons, and a concern for one family that is experiencing trials. Martha mentions a family in the neighborhood that has recently experienced a trauma brought on by a fire in their home. Several of the people indicate they have clothing and household items that could help. One couple declares their intention to help taking the suffering family's children to school during the next week.

Earl and Helen mention how important such help is in times of difficulty. They again thank the group for the help when Helen had emergency surgery. The couple remembers that the group came in and provided food, transportation, house cleaning, and clothes washing during the critical days. The group prays together mentioning these and other needs.

Robert asked if the family in need were believers. The answer from Henry indicates that they are not followers of Christ. Robert reminds the group that the help to the family is based on the natural response of Christians toward persons in need but also can be an avenue for sharing the Good News with them.

Mary reminds the group of the opportunity to provide needed items for children in Russia. The group briefly expresses the determination to grasp this service opportunity as well as praying for a church starter in Indonesia.

The group quickly turns to praise and Bible Study. Henry leads the interactive study of Scripture. Martha shares how she learned the spiritual value in maintaining integrity in the workplace where so much compromise seemed the way. Tom, a newcomer to the group, expressed his appreciation for the insight as he was facing the same workplace temptations to compromise and felt Martha's experience would strengthen him.

As part of their worship, the group commemorates the death of Christ by observing together the Lord's Supper. The group asked Henry to lead the service but the experience was actually a joint worship. The group completed plans for Don's baptism in the swimming pool at Henry's home the next week.

At the end of the period, the congregation continues the plan for a new group. Billy and Mary have been training to act as leaders for a new group. Two couples share their plan for beginning the new group in two weeks and indicate that two other couples have already shown interest in attending. Bill, a single man, expresses his interest in and commitment to a special group for singles–though he intends to remain part of the present gathering as well. The group remembers that their fellowship started as the outreach of two other house churches.

The period ends with prayer and fellowship between the people. Two couples leave quickly due to other obligations but several continue to speak together of the Lord and His work. All leave looking forward to the worship time next week.

Is the group described above a church? They have no building and follow local leaders. Was the observance of the Lord's Supper proper? Is it acceptable that this group actually approved and plans to carry out the baptism? Did the group demonstrate the characteristics of "church" and is it proper that they plan to enact the practices set out for a church? These imperative questions form the backdrop for the discussions in this book.

Definitions of Basic Churches

The gathering described above is one expression of a movement that is variously called simple church, cell church, organic church, or what this writer prefers, ***basic church***. These expressions of gathered Christianity are described as *a small group of people seeking intimate relationship with God and each other through hearing from God and living the Kingdom lifestyle*. For such groups, God is developing many different models and expressions of the Body of Christ. The important thing is that worship services, such as described above, are happening the world over, including North America.

In speaking of these local expressions of Christian fellowship, Dr. Daniel R. Sánchez indicates he prefers the term "basic church." Sánchez defines a "basic church" as one that carries out the basic functions of a New Testament church as described in Acts 2:40-47. In most New Testament passages, says Sánchez, the church is depicted as a local assembly of Christians who meet, worship, and minister in the name of Jesus Christ.[1] A basic church (simple church, organic church, house church, cell group) is, therefore, *a group of baptized believers who gather for purposes of worship and service under the leadership of the Holy Spirit and under the direction of the Lord Jesus Christ.*

J. D. Payne notes that the most critical issue facing the expansion of the North American Church today is the theological question. The important aspect of this question is, he says, "What is the church?" Payne continues that how this basic question is answered will impact organization, leadership development, evangelism, worship, and ministries.[2] Payne is correct. How we define church greatly impacts the evangelistic scene today.

Following Payne's pronouncement, our first step is to define the nature of church. Our theology must free believers to congregate in groups that are accepted as and have the rights to exist as churches. *House churches, simple churches, basic churches, and other expressions of organized Christian groups are churches.* They are neither less valid or less important nor more valid nor more important than other types of churches.

Such groups do not depend on buildings or denominational relationships. They may be a part of a movement or network that seeks to reproduce other congregations. Whatever the approach, these groups consider reproduction a vital, natural, and imperative part of their commitment. They are groups of believers who band together for mutual spiritual strength and for expanded opportunities to serve God. Frank Viola describes the basic church movement (not Viola's term) as "a largely hidden, yet growing stream of ordinary Christians."[3] Viola continues that God is using these ordinary Christians to summon back his people to the simplicity and vitality of the early church.[4]

Paul Kaak and Joe Boyd indicate that these churches that meet in houses (and other non-church building facilities such as offices, factories, conference centers, funeral homes, and etc.) are actually "missional outposts" or "missional communities of Jesus-followers."[5] John Payne indicates his support for the concept of basic churches by declaring that church planters must shift from an understanding of church that is based on cultural understandings and presuppositions.[6] Basic churches have the capacity for becoming a new force for reaching the lost and unchurched in the community. They can do this because they share the missional nature. Evangelism and church starting are written into the very DNA of these congregations.[7]

Basic churches, as they will be termed in this book, fit exactly into the category of missional congregations. Ed Stetzer and David Putman point out those congregations today must escape the "church culture" and impact their communities with the Gospel.[8] An important factor in Basic Churches is the fact that they almost naturally escape this "church culture" and relate directly to the communities they serve.

Robert and Julia Banks think that house churches have the characteristics of an extended family that involves singles, marrieds, and their children that meet regularly to address both the spiritual and non-spiritual needs. Mostly, these groups are missional outposts for spreading the Word of God.[9] In using the concept of the extended family, these leaders are thinking of the nature of the relationships between members and not restricting the congregation to any particular family group.

Nate Krupp indicates that his realization that ". . . it would take New Testament Christians to produce New Testament evangelism—and it would take New Testament churches to produce New Testament Christians" led him to consider the possibility of simple churches.[10] The insight into the possibilities of simple or basic churches led Krupp to the conviction that this plan of infinitely reproducible congregations would allow the fulfillment of the Great Commission.[11]

In a deeply theological work, Roger Gehring seeks to define a basic church or house church as a group that includes these elements:

- The group has developed its own religious life
- The group meets for worship, prayer, and fellowship
- The group accomplishes worship, evangelistic, and instructional proclamation
- The group promotes the celebration of baptism and the Lord's Supper
- The group may demonstrate some forms of organizational structure.

Gehring declares that the more visible these elements, the more certain we can be that we are dealing with a house church.[12] Wolfgang Simson adds the element of basic churches as fellowships in which the members teach each other how to obey the Lord. Such churches, says Simson, *do not have a message, they are a message.*[13]

Many approaches are more easily described than defined. The matter of basic churches exactly conforms to this assessment. In line with this view, Wolfgang Simson describes his vision for church as:

> . . like a spiritual extended family—organic, not organized, relational, not formal. It has a persecution-proof structure. It matures under tears, multiplies under pressure, breathes under water, grows under the carpet; it flourishes in the desert, sees in the dark and thrives in the midst of chaos. A church that can multiply like five loaves and two fish in the hands of Jesus, where the fathers turn their hearts to their sons and sons their hearts to their fathers, where its people are its resources, and which has only one name to boast about, the Lamb of God.[14]

Viola expands on the meaning of basic churches by saying that these fellowships are made up of believers who are willing to shed their man-made, encrusted traditions about church leadership, church practice, and church organization. These people, and the congregations they form, seek to hand the mastery of the groups back to the Lord Jesus Christ. These groups seek to recover both apostolic power and apostolic practice.[15]

An important aspect of simple churches or basic churches is the commitment to reproduction. These churches are, as Robert Fitts affirms, "born pregnant." The churches begin with the idea of reproducing and the expectation that each church will reproduce.[16] Larry Krieder insists that those leading basic churches in any form *". . . think in terms of our spiritual children starting their own house churches in the future."* [17]

The basic churches should realize that they will not attempt to grow to the point that they can start another congregation. Rather, these Christian groups think "reproduce" from the beginning. They turn their backs on any practice or idea that inhibits constant and continuing reproduction. Dave Browning in his book, *Deliberate Simplicity,* declares that churches today need to think decentralized instead of centralized and more instead of bigger.[18] Browing asks and answers an important question. How will a group that begins to reach out effectively accommodate the increasing numbers of people? The answer, states Browing is, "Either we find a bigger container to hold more people, or more containers to hold more people."[19] Browing, leader of the Christ the King Community Church goes on to point out that success, as it is defined by most of the Christian movement today, is often counter to genuine reproduction. This leads Browing to his conviction that more is better.[20]

George Barna, the noted Christian research specialist, boldly states that alternative fellowship forms (house church/simple church, post-modern churches, etc.), are currently home for 5 percent of USA Christians. These types of fellowships will, however, increase to make up 30-35 percent. Another 30-35 percent will live out their faith in the fields of media or arts and culture. The remaining 5 percent of Christians attending non-traditional forms of church will have a family-based spiritual life.[21] Many Christians will question Barna's prediction but must remember that he claims the 90 percent of his predictions in *Frog in the Kettle* have come to eventuality.[22]

Thom S. Rainer and Eric Geiger, who employ the term, "simple church," contend that simple churches usually are vital churches. These congregations follow simple processes of reaching and maturing people. "Simple churches," they say, "are making a big impact."[23] These authors define a simple church as, "a congregation designed around a straightforward and strategic process that moves people through the stages of spiritual growth."[24]

Basic churches look to the entire body of believers for service and ministry. These congregations avoid the deadening pattern of depending on paid and trained leaders who are often foreigners to the ministries in which they serve. These congregations maintain a worldwide vision as they seek to open opportunities for loving service. They maintain a commitment to and determination for unhindered reproduction. These ministries also stimulate Christian growth and service in the lives of believers. They have every right to be called churches. The Christian movement needs to affirm these congregations as fully churches.

Definitions of Church Multiplication Movements

A question related to the discussion of basic or simple churches often brings up queries about the methodology that has become known as Church-Planting Movements or as we prefer to call them, *Church Multiplication Movements*. Church-Planting Movements (CPM) are provisions of the Spirit of God in which churches multiply exponentially, unhindered, and in great numbers.

Church multiplication movements respond to the cry of Donald A. McGavran who, in 1965, declared, "What the fantastically multiplying populations of the earth need is fantastically multiplying churches."[25] Church Multiplication Movements provide the possibilities for these "fantastically multiplying churches." Walter Henrichsen is exactly correct in saying that while the world's populations are multiplying that churches are no more than adding. He concludes, "Addition can never keep pace with multiplication."[26]

David Garrison, who has led the effort to stimulate and attain approval of church planting movements, describes such movements as:

> . . . a rapid multiplication of indigenous churches planting churches that sweeps through a people group or population segment. [27]

Garrison points out that this definition underlines that such movements eventuate in rapid multiplication of churches that are indigenous (fit the communities they serve). These "divine miracles" are ministries that result in church multiplication.[28] He further points out that these movements consist of churches that themselves start churches. *It is this factor of local reproduction that permits the unhindered spread and infinite reproducibility of Christianity among and within a people group.*

Another part of the nature of church multiplication movements is that these efforts take place among a particular group of people, a people group, or a population segment. The quality of working within one people group does not deprive basic churches from reaching out to people and peoples different from their own. Each group has its own expressions of basic churches.

Finally, in his description of Church Planting Movements, Garrison speaks of the importance of such efforts. He says they are important because:

- God is working in and through them.
- God uses human effort in effecting the movements.
- God brings important results through them.

Garrison thinks that church planting movements

> . . . are the most effective means in the world today for drawing lost millions into saving disciple-building relationships with Jesus Christ.[29]

Basic churches often grow out of Church Multiplication Movements (CMM). For the Christian movement to be able to sustain CMM, many current but not biblical requirements for churches and movements must be discarded. John Payne states that "As long as church planters believe that our current cultural expectations for church are biblical requirements, the CMMs will remain impossibility."[30]

Questions about basic churches in many cases involve queries about Church Multiplication Movements. Are these movements congruent with biblical teachings? Are they valid methods for Christian missions? Do they avoid dangers that could blunt the outreach of the Gospel in days to come? Do they incorporate dangers to basic biblical teachings or practices? The answers to all these questions are yes. The negative answers that may rise from these questions should not produce a negative attitude toward these churches or movements. The positives far outweigh the negatives. In all likelihood, basic churches will most often eventuate from Church Multiplication Movements.

Strategies for Basic Churches and Church Multiplication Movements

In discussing both basic churches and Church Multiplication Movements, we must avoid the concept of "***the*** strategy for basic churches." In reality, no one strategy exists either for basic churches or for Church Multiplication Movements. The immediate situation indicates the direction of the strategies. While every method must pass the test of conformity to biblical teachings, these methods will be adjusted to meet local cultural needs in every case.

We should then, think in terms of strategies for basic churches and Church Multiplication Movements.

We should not impose overall requirements for groups to be known as churches, other than biblical foundations. The biblical teachings are all that are needed and all that should be should be employed. No one approach should be imposed. Workers should be encouraged to adjust the methods to the needs of their local situation without compromising biblical standards. This book does not call for abandoning all other approaches for the basic church method but does beg that organized Christianity fully allow this expression of congregational life.

Affirming Basic Churches and Church Multiplication Movements

The thesis of this writing is that these basic, simple groups and these movements of rapidly expanding and reproducing congregations can and should be viewed as Churches and as valid expressions of biblical Christianity. The methods are acceptable strategies and should be respected in every sense of the term. Basic churches and church multiplication movements are not the only expressions of gathered Christianity, they certainly constitute *one expression!*

This writing also strongly holds that movements of rapid multiplication of reproducing churches among a people group or population segment can happen, is happening, and will increasingly happen in North America.[31] One great opportunity for Christian outreach and service resides in the possibility of movements of church multiplication expanding across the world, including North America.

This writing agrees with Elmer Towns and Ed Stetzer who say that Christians in North America must accept and "bless" all forms of biblically sound churches be they large, small, multi-housing congregations, groups that meet in houses, groups with lay leadership, or cell group churches." These two writers declare, "We must learn to affirm the kind of churches that Scripture affirms." Towns and Stetzer conclude:

> If those who assemble together meet the biblical standards God calls them a 'church.' At that point, dare we see them as anything less than what God sees them? God calls them a 'church'.[32]

John Eldredge, author of *Waking the Dead* and *Wild at Heart* states his conviction that basic or simple churches are fully churches saying:

> God is calling together little communities of the heart, to fight for one another and for the hearts of those who have not yet been set free. That camaraderie, that intimacy, that incredible impact by a few stouthearted souls—that is available. It is the Christian life as Jesus gave it to us. It is completely normal.[33]

Ralph Winters concurs saying that the house church phenomenon could be not only revolutionary but also a valuable gift to the North American church. The basic church movement could renew the sense of family that God intended to be born in His churches.[34]

George Barna adds his words to the endorsement of different kinds of expressions of Christianity, both personal and corporate. Barna states:

> We must be very careful how we critique other people's spiritual journey. If someone's path conforms to biblical guidelines—even though it may stray from church traditions, cultural expectations, or our personal comfort zone—then we must accept the possibility that God may be working through him or her in a manner that is different than how He is working though us, or perhaps different than the ways we have previously seen or experienced His leading. We are called to be wise and discerning, but not judgmental.[35]

The Christian movement should heed Barna's words as they consider Basic Churches and Church Multiplication Movements.

This study defends the correctness of allowing The Christian movement to accept, consider, promote, seek, and approve basic, simple types of congregations to be churches in the fullest sense of the term. It seeks to gain acceptance of the strategies and methodologies that eventuate in simple or basic churches and Church Planting Movements (Church Multiplication Movements).

Fundamentally, this book advocates the acceptance of basic churches, Church Multiplication Movements, and the methods that these approaches involve to the extent that these movements follow biblical standards. These pages concur with the judgment of Del Birkey that the congregations of the New Testament were largely house churches.[36] The study is no attempt to set forth a systematic discussion of the doctrine of the Church. That study has been completed, wrapped up, and put to bed.[37] Rather, these pages give positive answers to a series of direct and crucial questions. The Christian movement should answer with a resounding "yes" these questions:

- Are “simple churches, or basic churches,” including congregations growing out of church-planting movements, churches that meet in houses, cell-group churches, and churches in multi-housing complexes *actually churches?* [Yes]
- Do these congregations reach and uphold the standards of biblical teachings in regard to being churches? [Yes]
- Can Bible-believing groups opt for, encourage, and allow these expressions of gathered Christians and remain true to biblical standards? [Yes]
- Are there requirements in biblical teachings that determine what kind of fellowships can be called by the name church? [Yes]
- Are the methods used in basic churches and Church Multiplication Movements acceptable? [yes]
- Is it possible that basic churches and Church Multiplication Movements allow a closer approach to biblical standards for “church” than some other expressions of gathered Christianity? [Yes]

This writing suggests one other question that should not receive the answer of yes. Are these methods demanded in the same applications in every situation? [no] Basic churches and Church Multiplication Movements are possible and efficient but not the only way.

A central group of convictions rests at the heart of what this writing is saying:

- We not only answer the above questions with an affirmative but will strive to establish the conviction that these expressions of Christianity are at least as congruent with the biblical teachings about churches as are some of the more traditional congregations that rely on buildings, professional staff, involved programs, and settled methods.

- We maintain that these organic, simple, basic groups are churches in every sense of the word and in many cases present possibilities for reaching a deeper level of congregational life and service than other approaches.
- We firmly believe that basic churches and other simple congregations that grow out of Church Multiplication Movements have the potential of allowing the fullest expression of and a more likely attainment of the meaning of *missional churches*. Missional churches are simply congregations committed to reaching the lost and unchurched through continuing evangelization and disciple-making.[38]
- We suggest that the Christian movement should *mandate the biblical requirements* of church and ***nothing more*** before accepting these fellowships as churches.
- At the same time, we are convinced that basic churches *are not the only method* of being biblical and effective in Kingdom service. This suggestion means that traditional churches still will serve and be served. The emphasis in this presentation simply is that we can allow for and promote both traditional churches and basic churches.

- We are convinced that we should allow and champion both the traditional church and the basic church approaches. Moreover, we should recognize that these methods are to be adjusted (contextualized) in each situation and not mandated in just one form.
- We are convinced that the phenomenon of Church Planting Movements (or Church Multiplication Movements) is a viable and needed method for spreading the Gospel around the world including North America.
- We believe the biblical concept of Church is a vessel large enough to contain many approaches and designs that can become "church" in the fullest sense of the term.

Discovering the actual meaning of church in the Scriptures brings the Christian movement to a decisive step. Too much of what the Christian movement has thought, taught, and insisted upon has sprung from tradition rather than biblical sources. To understand biblically what a church is and should be we need to:

- Study the biblical requirements for church *and require nothing more than these*
- Seek the basic meanings of the biblical metaphors for church and *embody and incorporate* these *meanings into congregations*
- Affirm the goal of congregations becoming *missional in the deepest sense of the word.*
- Focus on the entire world as they seek means of service and outreach

- Follow the biblical examples of biblical churches in action and *accept these findings in our thinking*
- Respond to the examples of present-day churches in action as they promote and *express the realities of church planting movements and basic churches*
- Answer questions about and objections to basic churches and *institute these concepts and convictions in life*
- Recognize and respond to the advantages that reside within the nature of basic churches including those dangers from which such congregations guard the Christian movement and *rest faithfully on these assurances*
- Analyze specific expressions of basic churches and Church Multiplication Movements to ascertain any weaknesses or unbiblical factors and suggest corrective measures to strengthen these congregations
- Commit to the starting, developing, and reproducing of thousands of basic churches around the world, including North America and accept and implement this ministry as a priority in the work of Christian groups. Accept various expressions of the methods of basic churches and Church Multiplication Movements
- Accept the possibility and work toward the implementation of Church Multiplication Movements. These movements, as is true of all Christian efforts, are attainable only through the direct action of the Holy Spirit. *We should pray earnestly for and not stand in the way of the Spirit's implementation of*

Church Multiplication Movements around the world.

We believe that following these guides to the meaning of church will allow us to fully accept and implement the concept of simple churches such as congregations that grow out of church planting movements, house churches, cell group churches, and other expressions of indigenous Christianity.

In the following pages we will outline the theology of basic churches and suggest ways that these congregations and the church-starting movements that they support can be experienced.

Let us evaluate groups of Christians, not just by traditional criteria such as special buildings, exclusive dependence on ordained leaders, accepted patterns, official relationships, standardized practices, or other accustomed matters. Let us name as church those groups that are made up of redeemed people that act like groups of redeemed people, that function like redeemed groups, and that seek the purposes and ends of redeemed fellowships.

Every Church (and church) continuously seeks to develop the capacity and characteristics of becoming missional. While basic churches will never be the one and only expression of Christianity, let us allow them to be a totally accepted and acceptable expression. Church multiplication movements are not the only way to reach a lost and needy world—but these methods are one way. These methods are proving to be an effective approach that the Lord is blessing in many parts of the world.

The Christian movement should adopt as its marching orders from the Lord the following determinations:

- *Accept and promote the possibilities of basic churches*
- *Accept and promote the possibilities of church multiplication movements*
- *Accept and promote the possibilities of missional churches*
- *Refuse any teachings or policies that restrict the unlimited multiplications of congregations*
- *Accept a variety of approaches to basic churches and Church Multiplication Movements—each adjusted to the circumstances while remaining fully within biblical parameters*
- *Set aside any teachings or policies that unjustly restrict or disallow church multiplication movements*
- *Commit to the possibilities and desirability of basic churches and church starting movements.*

CHAPTER 2

BASIC CHURCHES in BIBLICAL PERSPECTIVE

Basic churches (simple churches, house churches, small group congregations, cell-group churches, etc.) conform to the requirements for churches as these requirements are set forth in Scripture. *The Christian movement should follow the pattern of mandating* ***only*** *the biblical requirements of church rather than maintaining human-established lists of necessities.*

Church multiplication movements, when they conform to biblical standards, are fully allowed by biblical teachings and examples. Methodologies relating to basic churches and church multiplication movements should be fully supported, actively sought, and absolutely accepted by any Christian group that desires to see conversion growth and the increase in missional congregations.

Biblical Requirements For Church

Our thesis is that to express clearly the biblical pattern of "church," groups need incorporate only the following characteristics as seen in biblical descriptions of churches. The requirements for being a church are:

- Fellowships of born-again believers (Acts 2:41)
- Accept their fellowship as constituting a Christian church or gathering of believers under the Lord (Acts 2:41)

- Meet together for worship, mutual support, mutual training in Christian living, and service (Acts 2:41-46)
- Carry out the practices of church including the ordinances, service to God, ministry to each other, ministry to others, evangelism, worship, discipleship training, and transformation of the world (Acts 2: 47; 4:32-33; 541-42)
- Follow God-provided leaders who may be either professional or non-professional (Acts 4:23-31)
- Incorporate the total body into ministry (Acts 2:42; 4:23-31; 32-35)
- Reflect fully and faithfully the meaning of being the Body of Christ and the family of God (1 Cor 12: 12-31)
- Become fully ***missional*** in that the fellowship reproduces faithfully through reaching the lost and unchurched, serving the peoples of the world, and starting other congregations that also have the reproduction vision (Acts 11:19-30 ; 13:1-52).

Congregations will reach these levels of faith-living in several ways:

- *by responding to the basic nature of such an organism, that is, patterning after the Triune Nature of Jehovah;*
- *by engaging fully in the effort to enact the mission of Jesus by responding to the leading of the Holy Spirit to fulfill the mission of God in the world—through meeting needs and evangelizing people;*

- *by accepting their fellowship as church;*
- *by seeking to become the type of fellowship that can be described as family;*
- *by celebrating in their own fellowships the symbolic expressions of corporate worship, that is, baptism, prayer, and the Lord's Supper;*
- *by sharing with others all that God gives them (spiritual and material);*
- *by constantly seeking the lost and unchurched with the intention of sharing the Good News of Jesus with these needy peoples;*
- *by actively training both members and leaders in the processes of obedience-based development;*
- *by faithfully and intentionally achieving the trait of reproducibility both in the lives of members and for the congregations themselves;*
- *by becoming intentionally* ***missional****.*

Congregations that incorporate and demonstrate these characteristics are totally, completely, and authentically churches of the Lord Jesus Christ. These churches should be required only to conform to these biblical requirements of church. Churches, of whatever style or pattern should be expected to conform to these characteristics and not required to fit into other characteristics that often are man-made.

Basic churches may have neither special facilities nor professional staffs. They may follow various patterns of worship and service that differ from other congregations. They may set aside some traditional practices and incorporate some non-traditional ways. They may follow unique patterns for spreading the Word of God. *Yet, congregations should be known by the name "church" based on what they are and what they do!*

The most important requirement for a church is that it lives in accordance with its nature as a creation of God and a reflection of his love. Some have suggested that a church is what it does. *A better statement is that a church does what it is–it responds to its inner nature, its DNA.*

The usual requirements of it owning property, being in line with certain denominational principles, or having a large budget are less important than that the churches live out the mission of God that Jesus gave them. These fellowships are gatherings of saved people who make up a segment of the priesthood of believers.

A **missional church** seeks the lost and unchurched while avoiding the habit of spending most of its resources on itself. They take on the nature of apostolic groups. David Lyons, director of International Relations for the Navigators, urges simple churches to seek people from among the lost rather than from among the membership of traditional churches–in other words to be *purposely missional.*[39]

In *Shaped By God's Heart*, one of the more important books on missions in the 21st century, Milfred Minatrea defines a missional church as *". . . a reproducing community of authentic disciples, being equipped as missionaries sent by God, to live and proclaim His Kingdom in their world."* Minatrea points to the words of David Bosch and teaches that there is a "church" because there is a "mission," not vice versa.[40]

These definitions point to several imperative factors in a real church. The group is:

- a fellowship of authentic, worshiping, serving disciples (believers);
- one that is reproducing (in believers and congregations);
- one that is equipping its members as persons who spread the Gospel and minister in the name of God
- one that aims their witness and ministries at the world and the needs of its peoples.

A church need not be large, powerful, influential, wealthy, or well-known but it must be ***missional*** *else it is no church!* It seems obvious that basic churches are fulfilling these imperative functions. Clearly, these basic congregations, on these definitions, meet requirements for authentic churches.

We do not intend to suggest that large congregations with facilities, professional staffs, involved programs, expensive equipment, and large budgets are not biblical churches! This approach pleads only that we also recognize the small fellowships of believers, who meet in simple facilities (such as homes, businesses, schools, etc.) and follow non-professional leaders also fulfill the criteria for biblical churches so long as they demonstrate the characteristics of biblical churches.

But, how do we know what a church "patterned after the Triune Nature of God" would be? I suggest we go to the Bible and find what Jesus indicated his church would be! Ordinarily this means to look at those passages in Matthew's Gospel (Matt 16:16-20; 18:15-20). These are important words about the church. We are constrained to believe we should begin before these verses—at that seminal revelation from Jesus as to his ministry.

As the Body of Christ, the church is to reflect the missionary nature of Jesus and his ministry. This being true, we must begin with Luke 4:14-21. After Jesus defeated Satan and his temptations, The Lord returned to Galilee, received acclaim (and rejection) in the land, and entered the synagogue in Nazareth. The New Testament declares that:

> *He went to Nazareth, where he had been brought up, and on the Sabbath day he went into the synagogue, as was his custom. And he stood up to read. The scroll of the prophet Isaiah was handed to him. Unrolling it, he found the place where it is written:*
>
> *"The Spirit of the Lord is on me, because he has anointed me to preach good news to the poor. He has sent me to proclaim freedom for the prisoners and recovery of sight for the blind, to release the oppressed, to proclaim the year of the Lord's favor."*
>
> *Then he rolled up the scroll, gave it back to the attendant and sat down. The eyes of everyone in the synagogue were fastened on him,* ***and he began by saying to them, "Today this scripture is fulfilled in your hearing"*** *(Luke 4:16-21 NIV).*

With His reading these words from Isaiah, Jesus set forth the nature of His mission. He indicated that He had come to proclaim God's Good News to those who rested in need. He had come to secure release for those in bondage to evil powers. His was a mission of liberation and relationship to the Father (see Isa 42:7; 49:6-9).

We need require no more of a group to be called by the name of church today than that these fellowships be composed of believing, saved persons who carry out the mission that God gave the Son. Churches in the 21st century must engage in this vast ministry of deliverance from evil and restoration into God's family. *Church must be missional.* What was that mission?

Preaching the Gospel to the poor (Luke 4:14-21) involves far more than simply announcing orally the content of the Message. In fact, to limit the Lord's teaching to announcing the facts of the gospel (for example, the *Gospel Blimp*) is a miscarriage of the Lord's injunction. Proclaim means *to express, to make clear, to incarnate, and to share personally* the whole meaning of the Gospel with all people, including the disadvantaged. The recipients of this ministry include all those in spiritual need as well as those in physical difficulty.

A Christian or a church proclaims the Gospel to the needy only as that Christian or church bonds personally with the poor and needy, relates to them in their needs, and shares in their situation. This proclamation cannot be fulfilled by sending relief supplies—though this ministry should never be neglected. It demands hands on, personal attention. Proclaiming the Good News to the needy involves meeting both spiritual and physical needs—and the ministries grow out of the basic nature of the churches.

Proclaiming the Gospel to all people, including the disadvantaged, demands personal involvement. The example of proclaiming God's message to the poor is the ministry of Jesus who became involved to the extent that he "became *human and dwelled among us*." Biblical churches seek to become "incarnational" and communicate through the patterns that Jesus exemplified.

Proclaiming the Good News to the poor includes understanding the "poor" as those without the Gospel message as well as those without the necessities of life. No group that claims the name of "church" can remain separate from the obligation of the task of seeking the lost and unchurched and guiding them to faith in Jesus Christ.

The biblical requirement of being church is that of participating personally and incarnationally in the ministry of God through Jesus Christ as inspired and empowered by the Holy Spirit. A fellowship of believers that is so engaged should be given the name church. A gathering of people that is not proclaiming the Gospel to humanity in this incarnational way is failing to express the meaning of church in the biblical sense. Congregations of any size, who meet in any facility, who follow God-called leaders of any educational level, and proclaim by word and by deed the Gospel of Christ conform to the biblical requirements for church. *Let us require no more than this!*

Beginning our study of the nature of the Church with the revelation of Luke 4:16-21 does not mean that we overlook the important words of Jesus in Matt 16:13-20. The fullest meaning of this seminal passage cannot be approached in only a few words. For our purposes here, we note only that Jesus announced that his "church" would be built on the foundation of the faith confession that God had given to Peter. Peter's faith in Christ as the Messiah, the Promised Savior, came not from any human source but from the Father in heaven (v. 17). Jesus explained that on the foundation of such faith he would raise his assembly of the"called out ones," or the Church (v.18).

The church Jesus envisioned would stand firm in the world and never to be overpowered by the powers of the underworld, the agents of Satan (v. 18). Furthermore, the Church of Jesus is empowered by the gift of the "keys of the kingdom of heaven," that is, "the gospel in all its strength and power." The power of the Church allows the church to "loose and bind." Churches can forbid the un-biblical and allow the biblical because the Lord entrusts to his churches the dynamic and redemptive presence of God that is at work in and through his Church and his churches.[41]

Basic churches (simple churches, cell churches, house churches, multi-housing churches) are compatible with the biblical requirements for churches. These fellowships are:

- Groups of redeemed people,
- Who gather to worship and serve,
- Who accept themselves as expressions of the body of Christ,
- Who reach toward the nature of missional life,
- Who practice the ordinances,
- who serve the people in the memberships and communities,
- and who strive to reproduce in other congregations.

Why should they not be called what they clearly are—churches? The major question is not, do these groups conform to our preconceived ideas of what churches are but do they conform to the biblical teachings as to the nature of churches.

Biblical Requirements for Church Multiplication Movements

Church Multiplication Movements, in the contemporary sense, are not clearly mentioned in the New Testament. The fact remains, however, that in the experience of the New Testament outreach, one sees what closely resembles the phenomenon that contemporary leaders are calling Church Multiplication Movements. The account in the Book of Acts chronicles the vast addition of believers and the astounding multiplication of congregations as the Faith spread across the New Testament world. The explosion of outreach and the many territories evangelized in the early church period makes one think that something of a Church Multiplication Movement may indeed have taken place.

At least it can be said that nothing in Church Multiplication Movements contradicts New Testament teachings. These Movements do not produce groups that embrace unbiblical doctrines, practices, or features. The Church Multiplication Movements that Christians witness around the world are as free from doctrinal and behavioral problems as any other Christian efforts. The Movements eventuate in gatherings of redeemed people who then reproduce in other worshipping and serving groups.

The methodology of Church Multiplication Movements conforms to biblical standards. These movements reach biblical requirements for evangelism, church establishment, missional nature, and service elements. As we can accept basic churches as biblical and missional so can we accept Church Multiplication Movements as biblical and missional. *The methodology of Church Multiplication Movements is acceptable for Christians who believe the Bible and desire to obey the Great Commission.*

Conclusion

A requirement for any group to be a "church" involves that group actively participating in the Spirit-empowered mission of announcing and acting out the entire content of the Gospel that alone has the words of salvation from sin and incorporation into the life and ministry of Jesus. Congregations who serve in this fashion should be granted the title of *church*.

Movements that allow for unrestricted outreach Christians and Church leaders should greet the spread through new congregations with enthusiasm. Church Multiplication Movements represent acceptable methods for the 21st century just as were the God-empowered experiences in the 1st century.

Basic churches and Church Multiplication Movements are biblical, needed, possible, and doable in the 21st century. The Christian movement must not neglect these viable means of reaching the world and its peoples in this day. Christians and Christian groups should remove all obstacles from the staring of the needed new congregations and the development of imperative church multiplication movements in the United States and around the world.

CHAPTER 3

BIBLICAL METAPHORS of CHURCH

Basic churches and Church Multiplication Movements also conform to the biblical metaphors of church as seen in Scripture. Imperative insight into the meaning of church can be gleaned from consideration of these biblical metaphors of church. This suggestion is not to place further requirements on a group before that fellowship can be given the name church. It only suggests that additional light on the nature of these fellowships can be understood from the metaphors.

The New Testament suggests that churches conform to the metaphors of church. Please note the sentences in italics at the conclusion of the discussion of each metaphor as these sentences suggest some ways churches can ensure that they are in line with biblical principles that grow out of the metaphors of the Bible.

The Body of Christ

The metaphor, *the Body of Christ*, emphasizes the unity of the church as a group that shares the bread of the Lord's Supper (1 Cor 10:16-17). As the *Body of Christ*, the church is to live as a unified community in sacrificial love and fellowship—in a spirit of interdependence among all members. As the *Body of Christ*, the church is a full participant in the power encounter between God's reign and the forces of evil (Eph 1:22-23).[42]

One characteristic of a "body" in the physical sense is that of interdependence. The health of each part depends on the well-being of every other part. No one part of the body can fully function without the interplay of the other parts (1 Cor 12:12-31). Unity and interdependence are part of the meaning of the metaphor of the church as the Body of Christ.

A group lives in line with its God-intended nature only as it reflects this unity of interdependence and reflects the diversity of the gifts of the Spirit in its community life and service. Regardless of its denominational affiliation, its facilities, its trained and approved leaders, its recognition by the community, a group is only a church to the degree that it shows this characteristic of interdependence among its members.

The Congregation of Saints

Church is a fellowship of saved people, the *congregation of saints.* It is a new type of community (Rom 1:7; 1 Cor 1:2-3; Eph 1:1-2; Phil 1:1). The fellowship in the church is not something we bring about but is rather an expression of the church's nature. Only the saved can be and should be within the body of a church or the congregation of saints. While all humans are welcomed to any meetings and the unchurched the object of the love and search, the inner body must be composed of believers who join for worship and service.

A group lives in line with its God-intended nature only as it lives out its life as a fellowship of saved people. Any inclusion into the membership of unsaved people dilutes the group from being a true church. Any practice that admits unsaved people into the membership takes away the quality of being a church. Baptizing infants and including them into church membership defies this principle. A

church will, however, include the lost and unchurched in its love and fellowship as the congregation seeks to guide them into faith in Christ.

The Family of God

The image for the new people of God that Jesus called into being is the *familia Dei* or *family of God*. In this family, God is the father (Matt 23:9), Jesus the head of the household, and his followers are members of the household (Matt 10:25). The older women serve as mothers, the men as brothers, and the group together all serves as joint members of the household.[43]

Robert Banks has demonstrated that the Apostle Paul often used language that picked up the metaphor of family relations in his view of church. Paul indicated that those incorporated into the congregations should view themselves as members of a common family. Their relationships should be based on love and common care. They serve each other in the household (*oikos*). Church is well represented in the language that points out the inter working of a family.[44]

The centrality of the metaphor of the family of God in relation to the subject of basic churches can be easily comprehended by noting Paul's qualifications for church leaders. The Apostle noted that leaders should be persons who managed their own families well (1 Tim 3:5). This quality was important because the church closely resembles the characteristics of the family. Church leaders need the abilities to manage a household.

Actually this metaphor of the church as a family of God seems to reside in the very method of the early church. The group demonstrated the living reality of life in the

Father. The houses in which the groups met served as the foundation points from which outreach began. The elders in the house churches assumed exactly the housefather role.[45] Enlargement through the extended family pictures a main method of the spread of the Gospel in the first century. The mission of the Lord's early followers followed the house-to-house procedures (Luke 10:1-12).[46]

To the degree that a church reflects the nature of the extended family of God in its participants and worships it indicates that it has the DNA of an authentic church. Authentic churches take on the nature of effective families in their care of the parts of the body.

The People of God

The church is identified along faith lines rather than kinship lines. Life in the church transcends all political, racial, ethnic, and party relationships. Churches are expressions of the *People of God*. Only the church can bring genuine peace to people in the fragmented world (1 Pet 2:9; Rom 9:25-26). The church is a worldwide community that reaches to all peoples (Matt 18:19; Rev 5:9-10).

While local congregations may serve among a given population segment, the Church will be among every segment. Even those congregations that are primarily among one population segment will not demonstrate an exclusive nature but will welcome all and seek to bring all to faith. Churches will move in the direction of inclusiveness rather than promoting division among groups. These local expressions of the People of God have built into their very natures the commitment to reaching all groups of people everywhere in the world.

A group lives in line with its God-intended nature only as it transcends human divisions and tensions and reaches to include all people into the family of God. The People of God will not be divided my human animosities nor limited by racial or ethnic considerations. This unique fellowship is based on the unifying love of God for each believer and their consequent love for each other.

The Creation of the Spirit

Church comes into existence not by any human activity or power but only by the activity of the Holy Spirit. These congregations are *creations of the Spirit*. Church comes from the corporate nature of God's salvation (Acts 2:42-44; 1 Cor 2:16; Eph 2:19; 1 Pet 2:5). The plan for attaining the nature of a congregation is not some list of ten things that one must do but rather allowing the Holy Spirit to direct and empower the group for life and ministry.

Any idea of a human founder or human base of a congregation is foreign to biblical teachings. Churches are creations of the Spirit of God and not the result of human efforts or ingenuity. Every congregation must see itself as originating directly from the ministry of the Holy Spirit.

The parts of the fellowship share in ministry through the gifts of the Spirit (1 Cor 12:12-31). The congregation is acutely conscious of the fact that it is a creation of the Holy Spirit and never depends on human powers or abilities for its establishment, continuation, or power.

A group lives in line with its God-intended nature only as it grows out of the salvation experiences of its members, by the direct power of the Spirit, and through total reliance on the Holy Spirit for life and work. Churches are not the work of humans, are not born from human plans,

and never find life through human powers. The Spirit creates and maintains the basic church.

The Priests of God

The church exists to represent God to humans and humans to God. Church is *God's royal priesthood* (1 Pet 2:9). Church exists to inform people of God's love, reflect this love in service, and bring these people into God's Kingdom by witness through God's Spirit.

A church exists to represent God to people in the sense that the church expresses God's loving invitation to humankind. It will be a fellowship committed to the reaching of God's will in the world and for the world.

A group lives in line with its God-intended nature only as it serves as God's royal priesthood mediating God's love in reaching and ministering to others. The church, as the priests of God, stands between God and humans to prepare the way for relationships. This characteristic motivates the basic church to reach out to all and minister to them in the Name of God.

The Worshiping Flock

Church exists to praise and worship the God who created it by the Spirit. A basic church is a *worshiping flock.* Early Christians demonstrated their corporate nature by their joint love and praise (Acts 2 and 4). Worship is the active process of allowing the Spirit of God to enter and indwell the life of believers in individual and corporate meanings. Worship with a response is the type of worship a biblical church will experience. It will be worship in which the entire group joins and participates. It will be worship that results in action. It will be worship that exalts God and praises the Creator.

A group lives in line with its God-intended nature only as it actively, jointly, and passionately praises and follows God in heartfelt worship. The worship of the church not only praises God but also interacts with the Spirit to obey God and serve others. The outcome of the worship experience does not raise any person to prominence or praise but brings honor to God.

The Confessing Followers

Another metaphor of church relates to the church's confessional nature. Churches acknowledge Jesus Christ as the fulfillment of God's promises (Messiah) and the seat of all its ministries. It was Peter's confession that brought forth Jesus' statement about the establishment of his church (his little flock) (Matt 16:13-20). The Twelve represented the foundation upon which Jesus built his Church (Matt 12:22-40). The confession of Christ points to the center of the church's faith and determination.

A group lives in line with its God-intended nature only as it confesses BY WORD AND DEED its belief in and allegiance to Jesus Christ as its Lord. Confessing its nature leads a church to act rather that simply pronounce that Jesus is Lord. The confessing church witnesses to the relationship with God by the godly acts done by its parts.

A Living Organism

A church, in the biblical sense, lives, works, functions, and serves, as an organism. Paul taught the Corinthian Christians that in regard to spiritual gifts, a church resembled a human body with each part dependent upon the others and no part independent of the rest (1 Cor 12:12-31). An organism first is alive. It has that quality of life that separates it from all else that does not have life.

As an organism, the church also is a system of coordinated parts each of which has its distinctive and imperative function. Each part joyfully carries out its necessary function with thanks to God for allowing the service.

The image of the church as organism shows the tragedy of disunity or lack of commonality among the members of a church. A "church fight" is among the most disturbing misnomers of life. Churches, as organism, should live and serve from an integrated position of each part contributing.

An organism relies on every part for its healthy function. In a healthy church, every part of the body (each and every member) serves through the gifts the Spirit has provided and empowered. These churches incorporate every believer into the service of God and others.

It is part of the nature of an organism to divide and reproduce. A line of organisms will continue only as the individual expression of the organism produce more organisms that will also divide and expand. A church will, therefore, have as part of it basic nature the plan for, the determination to, and the freedom to reproduce.

A group lives in line with its God-intended nature only as it lives and serves through parts that mutually contribute according to the plan for each part, continues to demonstrate the qualities of life, and plans for reproducing other organisms or churches. Each part of the church (i.e. each person who is a part of the fellowship) contributes according to its gifts and received according to its needs. The church membership resembles a vast concert.

The Sharing Fellowship

A church corresponds to the biblical pattern as it shares all that it has with those in need; basic churches are *sharing fellowships*. It shares the new life in Christ. It shares the fellowship of its people. It shares the proceeds of its material possessions. A church does this, not because it is forced to but because its nature, its DNA, dictates this practice.

Any group that refuses or fails to share its living with all those in need is a group not demonstrating the nature of the church of Jesus Christ. A "non-sharing church" is a misstatement. Sharing physical assets is one important mark of a church that is congruent with biblical teachings.

A group lives in line with its God-intended nature only as it willingly, joyfully, and sacrificially shares all that it has with others (Acts 2:42-47). No member will experience need if other members have the capacity to meet the need. These churches will respond directly and willingly to the spirit of Eph 4:28. Christians in these fellowships will exhibit honesty by working at tasks that are beneficial to humankind for the purpose of having material goods that can be used to meet the needs of others.

Conclusion

A church in biblical teachings is a fellowship that conforms to the meaning and the spirit of the metaphors of church in the New Testament. The ministry of the church flows naturally out of the nature of the church. The church's nature reflects the mission of God in the world, exists (is possible) because of the redemptive work of Christ, and has the purpose of relating God's redemption to all of life.

Church exists as a social community that is both spiritual and human as it becomes a full demonstration of the new humanity and society in the world.[47] Small churches that meet in simple facilities under local leadership meet every aspect of the necessities to be accepted as churches on these criteria. Church multiplication movements relate directly to biblical teachings on the spread of Christianity in biblical times. Both Basic Churches and Church Multiplication Movements fulfill all requirements to be considered church, to be affirmed by the Christian movement, and to be promoted by those who desire to "make disciples" among all the peoples of the world.

The questions we raise about any particular fellowship or congregation is not in regard to its conformity to our traditional and accepted policies and practices but rather its conformity to the revelation of the nature of church in biblical teachings. *Let us not require more than the Lord does*. Let us never neglect a strategy that conforms to biblical requirements and holds great promise in Kingdom advance. Let us refuse to discredit or deny a method that God is using.

Basic churches and Church Multiplication Movements are obviously biblical and acceptable. While not the only method of evangelism and church growth, this strategy is certainly one way. ***The conviction of this writer is that basic churches are real churches and Church Multiplication Movements are genuine possibilities—in North America as well as other parts of the world***

CHAPTER 4

EXAMPLES of BIBLICAL CHURCHES in ACTION

Basic churches conform to the patterns of the churches in the New Testament accounts of the Christian movement. Attention to the examples of churches mentioned in Scripture provides additional insight into the types of actions, practices, and ministries of churches. A selection of passages dealing with the lives and ministries of churches described in the Bible reveals several important facets of the teachings concerning the natures of those groups who should be called "churches."

Characteristic Practices of New Testament Churches

Scripture speaks of churches and their practices in terms that support the understanding of basic churches. Scripture also speaks of the expansion of the Christian movement that supports the understanding of Church-Planting Movements. Based on these teachings, the Christian movement today is justified in projecting both Basic Churches and Church Multiplication Movements.

As we summarize these biblical teachings about churches, we will realize that basic churches or simple churches fully follow the examples of the practices of New Testament congregations. We also find that Church Multiplication Movements conform to biblical standards and greatly increase the worldwide outreach of the gospel community. Looking into the Scripture we find indications of the acceptability of basic churches and Church Multiplication Movements.

Churches in New Testament Teachings

These congregations were composed of persons who were saved by the grace of God and participated in the ministry of the Holy Spirit. They were "called out" from the rest of society to be the people of God (the meaning of the word, ἐκκλησία, is "called out"). The Jerusalem believers "gladly received the words of God" through Peter:

> *With many other words he warned them; and he pleaded with them, "Save yourselves from this corrupt generation." Those who accepted his message were baptized, and about three thousand were added to their number that day.*
>
> *They devoted themselves to the apostles' teaching and to the fellowship, to the breaking of bread and to prayer. Everyone was filled with awe, and many wonders and miraculous signs were done by the apostles. All the believers were together and had everything in common. Selling their possessions and goods, they gave to anyone as he had need. Every day they continued to meet together in the temple courts. They broke bread in their homes and ate together with glad and sincere hearts (Acts 2:40-46 NIV).*

Paul referred to the church members in Corinth as "the church of God that is in Corinth" and then described these believers as *"those who are sanctified in Christ Jesus, called to be saints," and as those who call upon the name of Jesus Christ, our Lord"* (1 Cor 1:2). Church, in the New Testament concept, was composed of saved people, and this characteristic remains as the imperative and unalterable quality of church.

These congregations continued without pause the Spirit-led activities of worship, prayer, joint-life (fellowship), ministry, discipleship, and witness (Acts 2:41-46). The Jerusalem Fellowship had purposes from which it did not turn. A church, in the biblical sense, centers on these purposes and not on keeping any tradition or set of traditions, not on any particular program or event or programs or events, and not on maintaining a building.[48]

These congregations fully proclaimed the gospel of Jesus even in the face of threats and persecution (Acts 4:23-41).

> *On their release, Peter and John went back to their own people and reported all that the chief priests and elders had said to them. When they heard this, they raised their voices together in prayer to God. "Sovereign Lord," they said, "you made the heaven and the earth and the sea, and everything in them. You spoke by the Holy Spirit through the mouth of your servant,*
> *our father David:*
> *" 'Why do the nations rage*
> *and the peoples plot in vain?*
> *The kings of the earth take their stand*
> *and the rulers gather together*
> *against the Lord*
> *and against his Anointed One. Indeed Herod and Pontius Pilate met together with the Gentiles and the people of Israel in this city to conspire against your holy servant Jesus, whom you anointed. They did what your power and will had decided beforehand should happen. Now, Lord, consider their threats and enable your servants to speak your word with great boldness. Stretch out your hand to heal and perform miraculous signs and wonders through the name of your holy servant Jesus."After they prayed, the place where they were meeting was shaken. And they were all filled with the Holy Spirit and spoke the word of God boldly* (Acts 4:23-31 NIV).

In the face of prohibition to proclaim Jesus and threats if they did, these disciples prayed only for one thing only. They petitioned God for "*boldness to speak* **Your** *word*" (Acts 4: 29). Nothing—be it threat or danger or inconvenience, or competing needs can ever dissuade a biblical church from fully and faithfully proclaiming, by word and deed, the total gospel of Jesus Christ.

These congregations faithfully maintained the true teachings and continuously sought God's will in the Scriptures **(Acts 2:41-42**). The doctrines of biblical churches come from Scripture and the leading of the Holy Spirit. No pressure from outside sources ever dictates to the biblical church what it must believe and do. This leadership comes only from the Scripture and the Spirit.

These congregations remained faithful in caring for their members in physical and spiritual ways as expressions of their joint-life in Christ **(Acts 2:44-47; 4:32-37; 2 Cor 8:1-5).**

> *All the believers were one in heart and mind. No one claimed that any of his possessions was his own, but they shared everything they had. With great power the apostles continued to testify to the resurrection of the Lord Jesus, and much grace was upon them all. There were no needy persons among them. For from time to time those who owned lands or houses sold them, brought the money from the sales and put it at the apostles' feet, and it was distributed to anyone as he had need.*
>
> *Joseph, a Levite from Cyprus, whom the apostles called Barnabas (which means Son of Encouragement),* [37]*sold a field he owned and brought the money and put it at the apostles' feet* (Acts 2:44-47 NIV).

No person in a biblical church had an unmet need. Christians in biblical churches gave sacrificially, without holding back, of their goods, to meet the needs of others in the fellowships. Christians in biblical churches gave not from their overflow but of their own goods to meet these needs (see also Acts 4:32-37; 2 Cor 8:1-5).

Church history reveals that the early churches cared not only for their own members but for others as well. In a letter to a Roman Government official, a lower governor indicated that the Christians were model in their behavior and also cared not only for their own needy but for others as well. Christians became known as dedicated and committed care givers.

These congregations existed in many places as local gatherings of God's people. Paul wrote to the church of God which is at Corinth **(1 Cor 1:2)** ***and the church of the Thessalonians*** **(1 Thess 1:1).** The local nature of these churches mentioned in Scripture is further seen in the probability that the Christians in Rome met in many small congregations each likely composed of believers from specific parts of the Roman Empire.[49] It is entirely possible that Paul's letter to the Ephesians was sent as a circular epistle to the many congregations in and around the central city of Ephesus.[50]

These congregations gathered in many types of meeting places—in synagogues **(Acts 18:4)*****, in homes*** **(Acts 18:7; Philemon 2; Rom 16:5)*****, in schools*** **(Acts 19:9)*****, and other places.*** The fact is that church buildings were unknown among the Christians until many years after the New Testament.[51] To make facilities a requirement for calling a congregation a church is much like making a nest a requirement for being a bird.

These congregations adjusted creatively with the cultures to which they ministered. Paul was careful to change the Jewish factors in the message to adjust more adequately to the Greek and Roman cultures of the churches in the Greek and Roman areas (Acts 15). He used Greek words such as "redemption" to express the true meaning of the Christian message. The Apostle John, when writing for a non-Jewish group, employed the Greek concept of "*logos*" to express the message. Importantly, the Apostles in adjusting the expression of the message never compromised the meaning of the message.

Is it not possible that cultural adjustment to the people being served is even more important to the characteristics of church than some more traditional aspects? Church, by its essential meaning, is a group adjusted to the service of its community. This means a different expression of church is needed for every segment of culture in any area.

These congregations followed the lead of local leaders, many of whom were not apostles **(Acts 14:21-26; Titus 1:5-7; 1 Tim 3:1-13).** Restricting church leadership to some form of ordination places an unbiblical requirement on church leaders. Frank Viola shows that the concept of a "covering," that is, an authority over one in the church, is basically unbiblical. Such a notion rests on a top-heavy, hierarchical understanding of authority. New Testament leadership, says Viola, is a functional mindset.[52]

Ordination, as practiced by many Church bodies today, may be one of the most unbiblical practices among us. Church leadership should be based on call and character not on ritual, ascribed position, or form.

These congregations freely celebrated the special services of baptism and the Lord's Supper. Paul declared that he had not baptized all the believers in Corinth (1 Cor 1:15-16) and instructed the Corinthians concerning certain improprieties in the way they were practicing the Lord's Supper (1 Cor 11:17-34).

These facts at least bend our thinking to the possibility that local leaders were presiding over both these church functions. We see no indication that the churches waited until apostles came to observe either baptism or the Lord's Supper. Biblical churches follow their own leaders in observing the special services of the Christian faith.

***These congregations practiced pastoral care and church discipline over their own members.* (Acts 2:41-42; 1 Pet 5:1-5; 1 Cor 5:1-13)**. Biblical churches practice church discipline on their local level with the goal of reclaiming fallen members, not in order to exclude persons from the fellowship. Pastoral care in biblical churches seeks to meet needs, correct behaviors, and stimulate faithful living and service.

Church discipline in the New Testament expressions aims at reclamation rather than separation. Too many churches have followed a pattern of expulsion in the name of church discipline. By direct action and by attitude these congregations have driven people away from the fellowship. Discipline aimed at reclamation is the essence of New Testament churches.

***These congregations constantly taught and practiced obedience to the Lord* (Acts 2:41-42).** The Apostles constantly called on the believers in the churches to grow in grace and knowledge and learn to implement the Christian life (1 Tim 4:15-16; 2 Cor 13:11; 1 Thess 5:23-24; 2 Pet 3:12-13; 1 John 2:28-29). The persons in the New Testament churches learned the "obedience that comes from faith" (Rom 1:5).

***These congregations were committed to missional ministry that included sending the Gospel to others, sharing to meet the needs of others, and reproducing in other congregations* (Acts 13:1-4; 2 Cor 8:1-24).** The churches of the New Testament engaged in an enormous ministry of missional outreach through discipling the lost and starting churches. Reproduction should be written into the DNA of every church. Biblical churches constantly seek ways to reproduce themselves. The goal of healthy church life and growth is gathering responsible, reproducing believers into responsible, reproducing congregations.[53]

We do not contend that every church in the New Testament period conformed only to the nature of a basic or simple church. We would, however, contend that the New Testament churches revealed patterns that basic churches today follow. The basic church pattern was not the only pattern in biblical times and it is not the one and only pattern for today. This fact leads us to consider basic churches as real churches and beg that the Christian movement accept these congregations as real churches.

Church Multiplication Movements in New Testament Teachings

Critics have asked if we can find examples of Church Multiplication Movements in the record of the early church. This record may not exactly describe what happened in the first Christian *century but the record does not rule out that movements like Church Multiplication Movements may have happened*. A study of the Book of Acts lends some credence to the possibility of a New Testament Church Multiplication Movement.

The Book of Acts records the rapid multiplication of churches that attended the explosion of the Faith after the event of the Resurrection of Christ. The Christian movement began with 120 (Acts 1:15) but rapidly mushroomed to over 3000 with the addition on the Day of Pentecost (Acts 2:41-42). After being arrested, threatened, and punished for their witness, the disciples prayed, not for protection but for boldness to proclaim the Gospel, and the company expanded to over 5000 (Acts 4:4). Later entries in Acts report that multitudes of men and women were added to the fellowships (Acts 5:14). The account could no longer be given in terms of adding but rather turned to the term multiplied in Acts 6:1-7. This increase came in response to the continuous witnessing of Christians, even in the face of persecution (Acts 8:4).

In Acts 9, the report begins to note the increase in the number of churches. The total number of congregations in Judea, Samaria, and Galilee are said to have multiplied (Acts 9:31). After Acts 16:5 the reports generally mention churches rather than church in tracing the Gospel movement. These data underscore the fact that early Christian growth involved the winning of converts and the planting of churches into which these converts were incorporated.[54]

Through chapter 9 of Acts, the Christian movement had remained largely within the Jewish people. In Acts 10 we see the movement to other peoples as Peter follows the Lord's instruction to carry the Word to the Roman, Cornelius. In Acts 11, the Gospel leaped the boundary of Jewish culture and began to expand among non-Jewish people in Antioch. From this congregation (or congregations perhaps), God used the Apostle Paul to spread the Word to Asia Minor, to Macedonia, to Greece, and finally to Rome. The record in Acts indicates that the Word of God continued to multiply (Acts 12:24), spread throughout entire regions (Acts 13:49), and grew mightily and prevailed over Asia Minor (Acts 19:20).

The Gospel had reached Rome before either Peter or Paul set foot in the city. Christians from every region had landed in the city and congregations were started. As already noted, theologian Paul Minear is most likely correct in saying that the church in Rome consisted of many small groups each built on one of the cultures from which the people had come.[55]

While not in the text of the Bible, traditions reports that the Gospel spread to other peoples through the witness of Christian travelers. Evidence for the existence of churches in Egypt, India, and Asia support the idea that the church expanded widely. The picture of early Christian expansion gives the impression of thousands of local fellowships multiplying unhindered and unrestricted across the world and among all the peoples of world. This description of biblical outreach sounds very much like a Church Multiplication Movement. At least, Church Multiplication Movements have no unbiblical or impractical elements within them.

Many of the reports of Christian expansion have the clear earmarks of Church Multiplication Movements. I would not claim that all Christian spread came by Church Multiplication Movements but would strongly suggest that some evidences of these types of phenomena were in place. While not insisting the all evangelism be by the methods of church multiplication movements, we would urge that these movements of the Holy Spirit be accepted and sought.

Conclusion

These teachings are not exhaustive. They suffice to indicate that churches in the biblical period did not possess facilities, ordained leaders, or requirements other than spiritual necessities for leaders. These small congregations actively practiced evangelism among the lost, development among the believers, worship for the saints, church symbolic services for the congregations, pastoral care for each other, church discipline when it was needed, and corporate life among the members.

What we see in the biblical teachings on the nature of churches, the metaphors of churches in the New Testament, and the examples of churches in the biblical period in no way mitigate against what is now being called "basic churches or simple churches." The simple churches fit nicely into the indications of the nature and examples of the churches of the New Testament period. In fact, many of these characteristics are actually more easily and naturally fulfilled in basic churches than in the larger, more organized congregations.

CHAPTER 5

PRESENT-DAY EXAMPLES

Basic churches and Church Planting Movements exist and minister in the world today. Church Multiplication Movements have arisen and flourish around the globe, including in North America. The examples of these churches further indicate the necessity of the Christian movement being open to and desirous of these expressions of gathered Christianity.

Examples of characteristics of basic churches and Church Multiplication Movements in mission history and in contemporary experiences indicate the necessities of these elements in basic churches and Church Planting Movements. While each characteristic may not be found in every movement, the congregations and movements together demonstrate the characteristics. Investigation of churches and movements across the centuries and in various regions indicates the characteristics of basic churches and Church Multiplication Movements.

Basic Churches and Church Multiplication Movements in Christian History

Most authorities agree that the early churches show characteristics of what today are called basic churches, simple churches, organic churches, house churches or other names. Many works chronicle the fact that the New Testament churches demonstrated many of the characteristics of basic churches.[56]

In the same vein, many writers indicate that the Early Christian movement demonstrated characteristics that are firmly in line with the natures of basic churches and Church Multiplication Movements. Wolfgang Simson shows the important place house churches occupied in early Christian history and in the mainlines of developing Christianity.[57] Such notable examples as Martin Luther's "third order of services," Jean de Labadie's emphasis on small groups (Conventicles), Philip Spener and his "pious gatherings," Wesley's cell groups, the house church movement in Great Britain, all demonstrate the relevance of basic church methods in Christian history.[58]

Mike Barnett and Dan Morgan trace the occurrences of phenomena that resemble what is now being called Church Multiplication Movements through Christian history. These professors of Missions show that such movements can be observed in biblical accounts as well as historical materials. They indicate present day evidences of these methods for church starting movements.[59]

These surveys of basic church methods and Church Multiplication Movements in biblical and historical sources provide foundations for present-day thinking on the subjects. Such reflection is imperative as the Christian movement for long periods has turned away from both methodologies—basic churches and CMMs. Wolfgang Simson recounts this "downward path" of retreat from basic churches and CMMs.[60] These historical facts in the preceding sources drives present-day church starters to consider strongly the importance of incorporating these methods into the contemporary expressions of mission. Can such methods be observed at the present time? Is it proper from a biblical perspective to start basic churches and encourage people to worship and serve in these congregations? The answers to these questions are yes. One reason for supporting basic churches lies in the fact that this approach conforms to the methods used by the early Christians.

Basic Churches and Church Multiplication Movements Outside North America

The Christian movement has rejoiced in recent years at reports of tremendous evangelistic and church starting results in many countries. These reports have come from around the world—Latin America, Asia, Africa, The Muslim World, Europe, and even North America[61]. On close examination, the incidence of these movements is found far more often in areas outside of Europe and North America. This section outlines in brief the incidence of the use of strategies of basic churches and Church Multiplication Movements around the world.

Among the Wallamo of Ethiopia

Missionaries came to the *Wallamo* people of Ethiopia in 1928 and after ten years of ministry, could count only around 48 believers. Political uncertainties forced the missionaries to leave in 1937 and in their departure could but wave to the small group of some 48 believing souls. The missionaries expected the movement to fail and perhaps disappear before they could return—if that day ever came.

The missionaries returned some five years later to find a far different situation than they had expected. The Gospel had, during their absence, spread marvelously. One of the *Wallamo* leaders stated, “When you missionaries left, it was difficult to find a Christian in *Wallamo* country. Now it is difficult to find a man who is not a Christian."[62] The believers reported that now over 100 congregations served the people and more than 10,000 believers were numbered among the populations.[63]

Christian observers can recognize several characteristics of basic churches and Church Planting Movements within the account of the growth of Christianity among the *Wallamo*. Among these characteristics are:

- The movement came among a particular people group
- The movement came through an expanding witness by Christians to the truth of the Gospel.
- The Gospel moved from person to person through dedicated sharing
- The movement grew without outside subsidy or the provision of church buildings
- The movement followed the leadership of local Christians who had no access to detailed theological training or reliance on any form of ordination
- The movement was free of any restrictive processes or regulations
- The congregations naturally and spontaneously reproduced by starting other congregations.
- The spread of the movement rested squarely on the work of the Holy Spirit and not on any human plan or operating
- The women were allowed to freely participate in the Gospel sharing and life within the congregations.

In the middle years of the 20th Century, the experience of the *Wallamo* followed something of what could be seen as basic churches and a Church Planting Movement. Of particular significance to the definition of basic churches and Church Planting Movements is the fact that this movement was among a particular people group, the congregations worshiped and served in local settings and not special buildings, the leaders were local Christians, and the congregations were reproducing. The Wallamo experience directly shows characteristics consistent with basic churches and Church Multiplication Movements. Christians in every area of the world can take courage from the experience of the work of God among the Wallamo.

In Tabasco State Of Mexico

In Tabasco, a state in Mexico, churches moved from a non-growth pattern to tremendous growth with the change to lay preachers and freedom of congregations to function as churches. The experience in Tabasco illustrates the vitality of a movement that relies on simple churches, house congregations, lay pastors, on-the-job leadership training, and complete body involvement in church ministry.

Evangelical work actually began as early as 1881 but experienced limited growth and development until 1935. Part of the background of the limited growth was persecution. An even more growth-restricting element, however, was the insistence of the Church and missionaries on culturally based regulations as to education of church leaders and the restricting of church leadership to ordained leaders (who were required to have education). In many cases, these regulations demanded bringing leaders from other areas of Mexico who were viewed as foreigners by the indigenous peoples of Tabasco.

Political events opened the way for a new experience for the churches and Christians in Tabasco in 1935. Leadership fell to uneducated, unbaptized, and sometimes persons living in common-law marriages to begin leading the churches. These men were unbaptized due to church regulations and unmarried due to rigid rules of the Church. The Gospel began phenomenal spread as churches and leaders emerged that were much more contextualized to the Tabasco cultures[64].

The experiences of the Christians and churches in Tabasco underline many values of simple churches and Church Multiplication Movements. Among these values and insights are:

- The importance of the Christian movement and the churches being contextualized into forms that fit the local culture in "everything not sinful."
- The importance of refusing to import regulations and means from outside an area and imposing these rules that so often can become growth-inhibiting elements.
- The importance of allowing local leadership to function fully as leaders of churches and to guide all church functions–including the church ordinances
- The importance of emphasizing spiritual matters rather than cultural matters in forming churches and selecting leaders.

- The importance of guiding Christians to live faithfully through persecution and difficulties

In Madhya Pradesh of Central India

Madhya Pradesh, a land-locked region in Central India, is home to over 70 million people who live in some six thousand villages. Even the urban areas of Madhya Pradesh are composed mostly of conglomerations of villages[65]. Dr. Victor Choudhrie, a prominent surgeon in India, followed God's call to evangelize and plant churches in this gospel-needy area. Leading an effort that closely resembles a Church Multiplication Movement and basic churches, Dr. Choudhrie has witnessed the Holy Spirit's blessing to the extent that over 4000 churches and more than 50,000 believers have arisen in this province. [66]

The movement shepherded by Dr. Choudhrie grew out of this leader's conviction that no human power could provide the number of church buildings needed nor maintain them if given. The churches in this effort were encouraged to meet in houses. The space for churches was already available. House churches were encouraged to begin, serve, and multiply.

The movement in Madhya Pradesh combined biblical teaching, lay leadership, and house church accommodations. These congregations remain totally separate from the "energy-sapping" dependence on foreign finances. They have no maintenance costs, no bills, and no salaries. These congregations and their leaders are free to concentrate on the church's main task—completing the Great Commission and making disciples of all peoples.

Experiences in Madhyua Pradesh in India demonstrate several insights important to the promotion of basic churches and Church Multiplication Movements. Among these principles are:

- The imperative of moving to an acceptance and promotion of simple, basic, house churches to reach unevangelized peoples
- The advantage of avoiding the influx of foreign funds and influences in indigenous movements of the Spirit
- The possibilities of lay, untrained leaders to guide the congregations
- The necessity of congregations multiplying without hindrances nor impediments.

In the Yanyin Province of China

In Yanyin Province (security makes the use of a pseudonym appropriate for this region) the lack of either growth or any real desire for growth among the established Church, led leaders to turn to the house churches. At the time, around three house churches with some 85 members existed in the province. As the Strategy Coordinator from outside the province encouraged and trained the local believers, growth began. In the first year, six new churches were established.

The second year, 17 more churches came into life and by the third year over 50 new congregations were born. By 1997 the number of congregations had jumped to 195 and the Gospel had reached every county in the province and each of the five ethnic groups. When the Strategy

Coordinator moved to a new region in 1998, the movement accelerated to the extent that the movement reached to 550 house churches with over 55,000 believers by the end of 1998. In the summer of 2001, leaders could count 900 congregations and almost 100,000 believers in Yanyin Province.[67]

This movement employed the strategy of mass evangelism often through the *Jesus Film*. Those directing the church starting efforts directed their witness to heads of households and expanded the outreach through family and relationship lines. Those who believed were immediately incorporated into basic discipleship studies and upon completion of these were baptized. The movement used multiple leadership in participative Bible Studies as a major method.

The experience in Yanyin Province reveals several principles in relation to basic churches and Church Multiplication Movements. Among these insights are:

- The necessity of turning from growth arresting and outreach limiting regulations and realities that may exist in traditional approaches to evangelism and church multiplication
- The importance of lay leadership rather than a continuing influx of outside leadership
- The imperative of allowing congregations to multiply without hindrance
- The need for consistent leadership training to provide the local leaders with guidance as they shepherd the congregations

- The expediency of directing evangelistic efforts to heads of household and along family lines
- The helpful strategy of participative studies that allowed multiple leadership in the congregations.

In A Cell-Group Church in Singapore

August 17, 1986 marked the beginning of the Faith Community Baptist Church in Singapore. Pastor Lawrence Khong guided the group in their first services and received an assurance from God that the effort was a work of the Spirit. This fellowship is a cell-group church. The church meets weekly in rented quarters for joint worship and ministry. The real life of the church, however, is acted out in cell groups that meet across the city.

Since the beginning in 1986, the church has grown until over 10,000 meet in the weekly worship events and more than 17,000 have accepted baptism. Almost every person who attends the worship services also is a part of cell group ministry during the week. In the small groups, the people are trained to minister the Gospel. A survey revealed that the giving to the church averages more than 25 percent of the church members' total income.[68]

Pastor Khong explains the difference between a church that has cells and a cell-group church. In the church with cells, such as Sunday School, fellowship department, ministry offerings, the cell ministries are only departments of the total church ministry. Members can select between the ministries. In a cell group church the primary ministries happen in the cells and the weekly gathering is a time of mutual help in Christian growth and living.

Cell groups are expected to multiply within 12 to 18 months as the result of continuing, member-involved evangelism. Any cell that does not multiply within a short period is considered unhealthy. Cells are never allowed to become inward-focused. These congregations view evangelism as their ultimate goal.

Pastor Khong draws on the insights of Ralph Neighbor Jr., saying that cells allow the church to penetrate society at every level. These groups remain in constant contact with the people around them and continue to influence by continuing evangelism and congregational multiplication.[69]

Cell groups often network with other cells to reach a particular segment of the population and to attain particular ministries. These networks allow for supervision in the form of help from the central church and from other cells. Workers often relate to several cells in sub-zones to counsel and support. The networking function links the cells into functioning entities.[70]

By contrast, in a cell-group church the cell is the church. The cells serve as the front door to the church. All resources of the church are designed to support the ministries of the cells. The cells, in turn, provide the structure through which members may become involved in church programs. Only members of the cell groups may join the training programs or Bible class of the church. Pastoral care is given through the cells and their ministries. Pastor Khong explains:

> When a person belongs to a cell, he or she is cared for spiritually, equipped for ministry, and mobilized for the preaching of the Gospel. In short, the cell fulfills all the primary functions of the church.[71]

The tremendous ministry of the Faith Community Baptist Church in Singapore testifies to the validity of such a church in a large, metropolitan area in the world today. The church also contributes some insights for those considering basic church and Church Multiplication Movement strategies. These insights include:

- Cell-group methods are effective in cities as well as rural areas. In fact, these methods hold the highest hopes for evangelizing and congregationalizing the cities of the world.
- Church development, even in more developed areas, does not depend on church buildings
- Cell group methods provide for the spiritual growth and Christian development of believers and also allow them to serve faithfully in God's work.
- Church can exist in various models and formats in different cultural settings. The cell-group church can more easily be contextualized than most models and thereby allows for penetrating into all levels of a culture and for reaching every population segment.
- Cells promote the *missional nature* of Christian groups by remaining continuously evangelistic and constantly multiplying. Healthy cells always look outward to the unchurched and never become inward focused.
- Cell group methods provide for networking and encouragement between cells. The sub-zone leaders provide guidance when and where it is required.

- Cells can provide for spiritual needs of persons and the world as these cells live out the commitment to Christ of their members.

The brief survey of basic churches and Church Multiplication Movements is but a sample of examples. Obviously, the Holy Spirit is active in such movements in non-western situations. But are such movements possible in North America? We turn to the questions of the strategies of basic churches and Church Multiplication Movements in North America.

Basic Churches and Church Multiplication Movements In North America

As a matter of fact, strategies that promote basic churches and Church Multiplication Movements are presently both evident and serving in North America. As expected, these efforts take some different directions and natures from those in other regions. These differences are due primarily to the differences in western cultures and the presence of traditional churches. Still, the basic characteristics of basic churches and Church Multiplication Movements are clearly evidences in North America.[72]

Attention has been directed in other books to movements such as NorthWood Church in Keller, Texas and Hope Church in Ft. Worth, Texas.[73] Networks of basic churches are erupting over North America. The conviction is that not only are strategies that use basic church methods and Church Multiplication Movement methods imperative for North America but are actually happening. The publication *House2House* gives continuing witness to these movements.

Mike Steele of DAWN provides an overview of budding Church Multiplication Movements in his chapter in *Church Planting Movements in North America.* Neil Cole points to the ministry God placed in the hands of his group, Church Multiplication. The group began with the idea that they would bring the lost to their churches. They received a change of direction from the Lord that moved them to take the message to the lost and unchurched people. The result was ten new congregations the first year.[74]

The momentum growing from this movement exceeded the group's expectations. In the second year, CMA started 18 churches. The next year 52 new starts were added. In 2002, an average of two churches a week was started resulting in at least 106 starts. In 2003 the group saw around 200 starts in a single year. Today there are probably more than 400 churches in 16 states and 12 nations around the world.

These churches were small (averaging 16 people) and simple. Cole summarizes this ministry saying that the group discovered the profound truth that if you lower the bar of how church is done and raise the bar of what it means to be a disciple, churches will empower the Christians to do the uncommon works of God. The result is churches that become healthy, fertile, and reproductive.[75]

Daniel Sanchez reports that McAllen, Texas has witnessed a church multiplication effort that is reaching unprecedented numbers of people with the Gospel. In 1994, says Sanchez, Armando and Maria Vera began a Christian meeting in their home with twelve participants. By 1996 they had grown to about 100 people and were holding worship services.

Not satisfied with this effort, Pastor and Mrs. Vera sought to lead this church to start a new congregation. Many people left the group because of a lack of vision, leaving Pastor Vera with only 46 members. This situation led him to begin to utilize house church strategies.

Since then, this church has started 65 new house churches (57 in the Rio Grande Valley, 6 in Mexico, and 2 in North Carolina).[76] While this pastor is utilizing a central congregation for its immediate community, he is committed to making a much greater impact by being instrumental in starting house churches everywhere that they have an opportunity to do so.[77]

As one reads the reports of Dave Browning concerning his congregation, the Christ the King Community Church, the description sounds very much like a Church Multiplication Movement. From a single stem, this congregation has moved to hundreds of congregations in the United States and other countries.[78]

Conclusion

These few examples demonstrate the fact that basic churches and Church Multiplication Movements are not strangers to North America. These strategies can be implemented in North America and are actually in the process of such implementation. The additional reading section of this book mentions numerous sources for information on and reports of the use of these methods.

This book does not suggest that we disband all traditional churches or cease using these methods. It simply calls for the acceptance of a new and highly effective means of reaching the lost and unchurched. It calls for accepting simple, basic churches as authentic churches and allowing them to flourish. It calls for mentioning that these methods are valid and needed.

Basic church methods and Church Multiplication Movements are possible in North America. The survey in this chapter but touches the total picture of such happenings. Churches and church groups in North America should adopt the concept of basic churches and Church Multiplication Movements, promote such churches and movements, and seek ways to enhance them. Basic churches and Church Multiplication Movements are happening, will happen, and remain immense needs in North America.

CHAPTER 6

RESPONDING to QUESTIONS

While Basic Churches are clearly evidenced in biblical teachings and while they have served throughout Christian history, objections to and questions about them surface often among Christian leaders. Those who advocate these types of fellowships and desire to call them "churches" should respond to these questions and answer these objections to basic congregations.

These questions and objections are clearly heard and easily understood as one listens to discussions concerning the nature of the small, independent, congregations that often differ from the larger, more traditional, and highly organized fellowship. By responding to these objections and questions, leaders of simple, basic, organic churches can improve both their service and their image in the Christian movement.

Are These Groups Churches?

Persons uncertain about basic churches often ask, "Are these groups actually churches?" The question addresses a number of concerns many sincere Christians and church leaders hold about basic churches. As seen earlier, these concerns most often center in concepts about the nature of churches that are not actually biblical requirements.

Nothing in Scripture indicates that churches must have buildings, denominational affiliation, ordained leaders, or legal standing. The Bible does not require every new congregation have a "mother church." No denominational DNA is mentioned in the New Testament. The question about the legitimacy of these congregations as churches arises primarily from non-biblical sources, traditions, and concerns.

The conviction of these writers is that Basic Churches, by whatever name one calls them, are real, genuine, churches. They are compatible with biblical teachings concerning church. They do what churches do! I agree with John Payne that a change from traditional convictions about the nature of churches to new and more flexible patterns is the first shift necessary for the Church today.[79]

The foregoing chapters have attempted to set out the biblical requirements for a congregation to be known as a biblical church. These chapters have declared that the basic churches fulfill these requirements. These Basic Churches, many of which grow out of Church Multiplication Movements, are fully churches and should be accepted as such.

Will These Groups Maintain Biblical Theology?

Christians are understandably and properly concerned about true doctrine. Theological error has led and continues to lead to many problems within the Christian Movement. Such concern has led many to question the possibility of avoiding doctrinal deviation in many small congregations that are not closely supervised by some authority. Frank Viola shows that a large part of the emphasis on the unbiblical concept on "covering" (that is, having an authoritative supervisor over the church and its leaders) springs from the fear that such groups will compromise Christian teaching.[80]

Often the cry is that basic churches will open the door to false teachings and that doctrine and practice in these congregations cannot be controlled. *Many of the most destructive heresies in the teachings about the doctrine of the church and the ministry of the churches have arisen from efforts to safeguard the doctrinal purity of the Christian movement (e.g.., Council of Trent).*[81] Wayne Jacobsen points out that basic churches do not foster theological error. In fact he says that over the past 2000 years, most heresy has arisen within the organized Church from "leaders" who thought they understood God's mind better than anyone else.[82] The basic churches have not been seedbeds of theological error.

Among Indonesian Baptists in the 1970s, the plan to start 1000s of small house churches was met by this question. Some pastors expressed the fear that in such congregations there would be no way to ensure doctrinal integrity. This line of questioning has arisen in many different locations and situations over the years.

The fact is that doctrinal error has often, in Christian history, arisen from the authoritative Church organization rather than in basic type churches. A central power with coercive ability does not assure doctrinal stability. Theological error can and does arise in many different organizational types. John Arnott expresses his conviction that the Church of Jesus Christ better fulfills its mission and remains faithful to its calling in small congregations than in the situation where Church assumes political and hierarchical perspectives.[83]

Basic churches are as likely as any other type to maintain doctrinal integrity. In some ways, they may be less influenced by theological drift than those congregations more aligned with denominational realities. Faithfulness to biblical teachings rests more on spiritual vitality than on Church authority.

No genuine evidence exists to suggest that Basic Churches have a greater tendency toward theological error than more traditional congregations. Doctrinal integrity can be attained by carefully proclaiming the true Gospel to those who are evangelized and faithfully guiding them in discipleship (Jude 3).

The Apostle Paul maintained close watch care over the congregations he started and warned when false teachings arose. The epistles of the New Testament contain many warnings about false teachings and teachers. The anxiety over doctrine is well founded. Any Church Multiplication Movement should incorporate some means to protect the biblical core of doctrine.

Will These Churches Have Biblical Leaders?

Leadership for churches is vital. A reasonable question arises as to the source of leaders for basic churches and Church Multiplication Movements. Most mission groups seek to supply this need by starting some type of pastor training early in their ministries in a region. This provision leads either to the rule or at least to the tradition that only those who have received the training should be leaders of the churches.

The fact is that local leaders can and should guide the congregations. These leaders will need training but can receive it "on the job" rather than at a training school. Local leaders already have respect and position in the communities and can lead effectively. The leaders receive confirmation from the congregations they lead. Paul set apart leaders in the churches he started and left leadership in their hands. The Apostle did, however, find it necessary to correct some incorrect teachings and practices from time to time (1 Cor 3:1-23; Tit 1:10-16).

The problems with the training school approach are varied. One, the prospective leader is usually removed from his location. Two, an artificial environment is created and the experience in these environments often further divides the leader from the membership. Third, the training schools usually cannot keep up with the needs.

Movements that depend on local, lay leadership and provide training within the community allow for unhindered multiplication. There is no need for delaying the beginning of a new church until a graduate of the training school is available. Local leaders often show a maturity not yet attained by the younger people who can leave home and travel to the training school.

Basic Churches require leadership. Movements seldom bloom without definite and positive leaders. This leadership, however, can and usually should be local, lay leaders. Only by incorporating the concept of local, nonprofessional leadership can Church Multiplication Movements be realized. Leadership is available when the congregation looks to its own resources to provide the guidance and not to incorporating leaders from other groups. Leaders will arise for Basic Churches and will guide the congregations in biblically acceptable ways.

Will These Groups Properly Observe the Ordinances?

Questions also arise as to the propriety of these basic churches observing the Christian ordinances of baptism and the Lord's Supper. These ordinances have been conceived to be strictly church ordinances that must be presided over by ordained leaders. The Christian movement must safeguard the integrity of the church ordinances. Authority for these worship services should be in the congregation not the leader. The congregations must avoid the corrosive results of self-serving leaders.

Some years ago a missionary addressed a group at a summer missionary week and explained his problem of being overworked. He explained that in the area in which he was serving, he was the only ordained minister among a group of over twenty churches. This situation, he said, forced him to travel almost weekly to some church to lead the service of the Lord's Supper. The question immediately surfaced in some minds as to why the local church leaders could not administer this worship service.

At another missionary meeting, the question arose as to how new believers could possibly be baptized in a New Testament fashion. The problem, according to a missionary, was that no ordained ministers were present to administer what the missionary considered "biblical baptism." The question arose in some minds—why not allow the natural leaders of the groups to perform the service of baptism.

While baptism and the Lord's Supper definitely are church ordinances, no real evidence suggests that the New Testament required professional, ordained leaders to preside over them. In fact the opposite seems to have been the apostolic pattern. As seen, the Apostle entrusted leadership of the congregations to leaders from the existing congregations. Insisting that only ordained leadership can administer the church ordinances moves away from New Testament patterns.

Restricting the ordinances to established, official churches and to the leadership of trained, professional, ordained leaders rests among the most harmful heresies of the Christian movement. Nothing is wrong with observing the ordinances in established congregations with ordained leaders. What is harmful is restricting the ordinances to the established churches and requiring ordained leaders for their observance.

Basic Churches and their local leaders should be allowed and encouraged to observe the church ordinances. These congregations have authority to oversee both baptism and the Lord's Supper. Denying these congregations and their leaders this right hinders the expansion of the movements and lessens the dynamic quality of the local churches. Unlimited reproducibility demands unlimited access to the worship of the church ordinances. This principle is important to the experience of small group evangelism and church development.

Do These Groups Incorporate and Disciple Members?

Questions about incorporation of members and the maturing of members arise in relation to basic churches and Church Multiplication Movements. Some question the correctness of such groups actually granting church membership. Under such views, members in churches that are new and not established by some formal means, are often considered members of some other church—perhaps the sponsoring church. In a certain mission field, the first converts were baptized into a church in the United States.

This question can be answered from the perspective that the Bible does not require a church to be official or established before believers can become part of the fellowship. No reason exists to refuse to call these believers members of the church. Basic Churches may have better possibilities of incorporating new members than larger, more established congregations.

As to discipleship, the basic church is as likely to be able to guide new believers in Christian growth as the larger, more established congregations. In fact, the small near-by fellowships made up of friends and neighbors, provides natural guidance in Christian living. The Basic Churches have a built-in capacity to guide people in Christian growth because they have more intimate relationships with the new believers.

Incorporation and discipleship can and should be achieved in basic churches. The participants in basic churches teach each other the ways to Christian obedience. Christian growth is a more natural step as this increase happens within a group setting where natural oversight, stimulation, and guidance is possible. Basic churches should, and have been observed to do so, guide people in spiritual growth and development.

Can Such Groups Adequately Proclaim the Gospel?

Some ask if the basic churches can adequately proclaim the full gospel. A corollary question sometimes asks if these churches participate in Great Commission Missions—sending the Gospel to other groups. Robert and Julia Banks indicate that some people ask if house churches encourage people to focus on spiritual and relational concerns at the expense of effective outreach and mission.[84]

These small churches, suggest some leaders, do not have the strength or facilities to provide for the complete proclamation of the Gospel. They have no access to some of the modern technological means for spreading the Message. They do not have trained leaders to adequately express this Message.

Gospel proclamation does not depend on technological materials or advanced training. The Gospel, as presented in the Bible, is simple and can be proclaimed in simple ways. Lay leaders are not limited leaders. Many have advanced training is some fields. They can, under the leadership of the Holy Spirit, proclaim the Gospel, by word and by deed, so that the world can hear.

As Robert and Julia Banks show, house churches do not limit missional intent or activity. As well-functioning families, these groups equip their members to look outward for evangelism and ministry. House churches do not characteristically become inward looking or cliquish. These expressions of gathered Christianity encouraged their members to reach out and win those who are unchurched.[85]

Basic churches do not limit Gospel proclamation. In fact, these congregations, by stimulating the unhindered spread of the word from person to person, enhance the fulfillment of the Great Commission. The fact that Church Multiplication Movements have for the most part been active among persons in non-western environments suggests that this method holds great validity as a means of cross-cultural missions. The opposite truth is, however, that these methods are valid in North America as well.

Will These Groups Become Missional Churches?

As seen earlier, missional churches are congregations made up of authentic disciples of Christ, that are reproducing by reaching new believers, starting new groups, equipping disciples to serve God, and achieving these ministries in the world where God places them. Do the Basic Churches, meeting in homes and other places, led by lay, unordained leaders, having only the most basic organizations, having little denominational attachment, qualify as missional churches? Lawrence Khong adequately answers this question in his discussions of the cell groups in Faith Community Baptist Church (see chapter 4).

Larry Kreider strongly asserts that the house churches should focus on outreach and discipleship. Great fellowship will naturally flow from this emphasis. The close fellowship will come as a byproduct of group constantly reaching out to others evangelistically and in ministry.[86]

We think, therefore, the answer is yes. These congregations are composed of authentic believers who are active in reaching others for Christ. These congregations equip the members for their missionary activities in witness and service. These congregations are fully active in reproductive efforts—both in believers and groups. These congregations have leaders and often join with others in networks for mutual help and stimulation. They are certainly *missional* in every sense of the concept.

Basic Churches, meeting in homes, striving to reproduce by cell division may more easily attain to the characteristics of missional than other kinds of churches. The Christian movement should support these congregations, acknowledge them, and promote their ministries. In basic churches the Christian movement may see a return to New Testament type expansion.

Do These Groups Properly Seek to Transform People and Societies?

Some have questioned the abilities of house churches or basic churches to properly impact society and the world with the full and changing power of Christ. The concern is valid. Basic Churches do not shun the hard work of transforming both people and the societies in which they live. Basic Churches realize the church and mission cannot be separated.[87]

Basic Churches see themselves as under obligation, as people of God, to reach out to the spiritual and physical needs of the people in the communities the group serves. Should a group fail in the missional functions of outreach and service, the reason will be unfaithfulness to the commission rather than the fact that the group is a basic church. Failure of missional practices is not limited to basic churches. In fact, missional practice is enhanced in the small groups of Basic Churches. Basic churches can and should seek to change the society in directions that are congruent with biblical teachings.

Conclusion

As seen in the discussions above, each of the questions can be answered affirmatively. These groups are fully biblical churches, led by God-called and faithful leaders, uphold biblical doctrine, proclaim the Message, win and disciple members, and participate in the Great Commission. The questions are understandable and should be considered thoughtfully. We have tried to do just that! We do not disregard the questions and the anxieties that lie behind them. We are convinced, however, that the questions can and have been answered and the anxieties put at rest.

CHAPTER 7

THE ADVANTAGES of BASIC CHURCHES

Hopefully, we have conveyed the thought that basic churches and church multiplication movements are but two of the methods that can help reach the goal of world evangelization. This book is certainly not a call to stop all other efforts and simply follow these. The call is here to allow and encourage these methods as proper and acceptable.

Some question the propriety of designating as "church" smaller congregations that meet in simple facilities, follow voluntary, non-professional leaders, and deviate from traditional patterns. The actual fact is that Basic Churches and congregations growing out of Church Multiplication Movements, cell-group churches, house church patterns, and efforts in multi-housing settings provide safeguards against some of the most damaging tendencies within the Christian movement. *Rather than constituting a danger for the Christian movement, basic churches provide advantages and safeguards for Christian development.*

Allowing and promoting small groups as totally acceptable and fully functioning as churches, the Christian movement can, therefore, avoid some of the more devastating "unbiblical" patterns that have emerged in Christian history. By affirming Church Multiplication Movements, the Christian Church can avoid the deadening problem of arrested development.

In actual fact, Basic Churches and Church Multiplication Movements present far more advantages than disadvantages. These movements provide protection against some of the major growth-inhibiting factors in Christian outreach. We turn now to the advantages which the basic church methodologies help protect.

Providing Structure Without Hierarchical Control

Basic Churches and Church Multiplication Movements provide stability in the fellowship that naturally grows between congregations but avoids the problem of hierarchical, centralized power. One of the more damaging heresies of Christian history is "The Hierarchical Church." The Hierarchical Church has assumed power over salvation and taken the right to dispense, withhold, or withdraw eternal life.[88] Avoiding the heresy of the Hierarchical Church is a definite advantage of basic church strategy.

This situation would not have arisen if the emphasis had remained on the local congregations. A hierarchical Church that has coercive power opens the door to endless errors. Christian history demonstrates that the rise of a universal, hierarchical, controlling, and all-powerful Church leads to a pattern of errors that include:[89]

- Moving away from salvation by grace to salvation through the Church
- Placing works, often in the guise of Church rituals, in the way of genuine salvation
- Creating a special category of leaders with unique positions, dress, requirements (celibacy), canonization of "saints," restriction of the Bible and Lord's

Supper cup from laity, and the creation of the papacy

- Enabling leadership to exert coercive power and domination that is totally foreign to the leadership plan of Jesus (Matt 20:24-28)
- Leading to false teachings such as emphasis on Mary, images and relics, purgatory, dogma of the sacraments, indulgences, and giving of authority to Church tradition that was equal to the Bible[90]
- Opening the door for religious persecution and oppression
- Restricting multiplication of congregations
- Leading to a hierarchy within the Body that eventually weakens the entire organism and even threatens collapse.
- Weakening the major strength of the Body by giving to the professional staff the responsibility of performing ministry and thereby failing to equip and engage the entire Body
- Focusing on maintaining the organization, doctrine, and status of the Church rather than making disciples of men and women
- Denying the creativity of newer forms of Christian expression by demanding conformity to the Church's standard beliefs and practices.

Mandating only the biblical requirements of church also avoids the error of establishing a heirarchialism that allows leaders from the top to dictate to the congregations what they must believe and practice. This hierarchialism often creates the climate for controversy and coercion. When any group of churches (association, denomination) becomes embroiled in controversy over basically secular concerns or when any group uses basically secular means to attempt to dominate that Church or church, that group has ceased to demonstrate the qualities of a church living out New Testament principles. Requiring only biblical elements in churches can help avoid such an error.

Avoiding the Universal, Central Church pattern must receive a high priority from those concerned with a biblical expression of Christianity. Stability and accountability among congregations can be achieved through networks of basic churches. These networks, while not authorative, demanding entities can give aid and direction to basic churches. Basic churches promise the avoidance of this problem while at the same time allows sufficient structure for the Christian movement.

Providing Adequate Leadership Without Professional Leaders

The patterns basic churches and church multiplication also avoid the error of allowing ***only*** *an ordained, professional leadership.* This method creates a governing power that stands different from the rest of the Body—having different functions, vestments, titles, privileges, and honors. Professional, ordained leadership has contributed much to the advance of Christianity over the centuries.

Depending exclusively on professional, ordained, hierarchical leadership is, however, a *major heresy* that has arisen in Christian history. The biblical way is for church leadership to be servant leaders who equip the Body (the entire membership) to employ their particular spiritual gifts in the ministry of the Lord (Eph 4:11-16). Church leaders should not perform; they should equip others to do the task.[91]

The above pattern clearly follows the biblical way the Apostle outlined in Ephesians. This passage indicates that the Lord gives the leaders to the church. The Lord then commissions these leaders to equip or prepare the body of Christ, that is, the members, so that they can perform the works of ministry. It is by these works that the body itself will be built up, reach unity, and attain maturity. The body will never mature properly if the leadership does the work.

Clearly the biblical pattern requires for God-called leaders to equip the entire body *for the performance of the Holy Spirit empowered services. Restricting any ministry in the church to those who have some denominational entitlement or credentials is heresy.* Insisting on only a trained, ordained, approved leadership restricts the unlimited multiplication of churches and their uninhibited ability to serve. Speaking biblically, every church should have within its membership persons who can, are expected and are allowed to carry out every function the church needs to promote.

Dave Browing almost surprises us in speaking of leadership. He calls leaders in his group, "pastorpreneurial" leaders. He defines these persons as a kingdom-mined leader who has a heart for people (pastor-) and the ingenuity to reach them (-perenurial). A pastorpreneur has received God both the heart and the head, the sensitivity and the skills to make a difference. Perhaps even more surprising, Browing indicates that the procedure among his network of churches is that the church identifies the leaders, then deploys them, and when they are in the game, trains them.[92]

Churches growing out of Church Multiplication Movements, house churches (cell groups), and multi-housing ministries provide a safeguard against the development of such restrictions that place power and service only in the hands of the "ordained ministry." This book does not call for doing away with the professional, ordained ministry but simply allowing the practice of ministry by the local leaders. The approach suggested does not call for disbanding all formal expressions of church. These words simply beg that simple churches be added to our concept of church and allowed to thrive.

Providing a Platform of Missional Churches

Basic churches of several types provide an adequate platform for missional churches. Many of the characteristics that hinder other types of churches from becoming missional are not found in basic, simple churches. It is a fact that many new churches stall when they attain the level of a building. The building, the necessary maintenance and payments, consume most of the church's resources. Rather than thinking reproduction, these churches often think maintenance. The missional nature is lost in the mix.

Basic churches, on the other hand, are free from the financial needs of their more organized brother and sister congregations. Churches that do not feel the need to enhance their facilities, their statuses, and their positions do not so easily develop unbiblical patterns of spending on themselves rather than on others. Basic churches can, therefore, more easily engage in activities that enhance missional qualities. Such churches that look toward extensive reproduction and service to their communities are willing to place their energies and possessions into missions of reproduction.

Denominational regulations are not a hindrance to basic churches but do sometimes hinder traditional churches in their development. Traditional patterns are often forced to commit more and more resources to keeping the organism alive. Basic churches, free of such needs, can devote themselves to the task of world evangelization and community service.

Further, basic churches can concentrate on direct ministry. The needy are touched in incarnational ways by these Christians groups. The very DNA of these congregations drives them to meet direct human needs in their communities and then extend these services to other communities.

Basic churches can provide this foundation for missional nature. Some simple churches may fail to achieve this goal. Many more traditional congregations will become fully missional. The missional nature will not be in only one expression of Christianity. Still, the basic foundation rests within basic churches to become missional and the great possibility is that these congregations can and will become missional churches.

Creating a Climate for Total Church Ministry

The strategies connected with basic churches create a climate for the ministry of the entire church. The vision of Eph 4:11-13 can be reached. Ministry ceases to be the responsibility of a few, authorized persons and becomes the opportunity for the entire body—that is, all the believers.

The opening for total body ministry provides two important factors. First, the work gets done. The limitation of time and relationship that is most often present in traditional pastoral/people models disappears in the service of all believers. Pastoral care increases rather than decreases.

The second provision of total body ministry is the development of the spiritual life of the believers. Direct service in the Lord's work is the finest discipleship method known. When believers participate in evangelism and discipleship efforts, they grow more fully and develop more deeply. Further, basic churches guide in training believers in obedient Christian living.

The goal in these congregations is not increasing knowledge and understanding (although these functions are recognized and sought) but rather helping people increase in their dedication to obedience to the Lord and His purposes. The members of basic churches aid each other in reaching the "obedience that grows out of faith" (Rom. 1:5).[93]

Basic church strategies provide for ministry and for Christian growth. God's work is accomplished by the efforts of God's total people. These strategies allow for reaching the unchurched and developing the believers.

Providing a Persecution-Proof Environment for Believers

Wolfgang Simson speaks directly of the advantage of basic churches and house churches in the face to persecution. Simson is not suggesting that the churches seek to flee or escape persecution. After all, persecution has never in the past and will never in the future destroy the witness of Christ. We must seek to be worthy of suffering for the name and work of Jesus.[94]

Because of the flexible structure and inner strength of the basic churches, they allow the Gospel to continue to expand even in the face of persecution. The very fact that these churches have no buildings helps insulate them from some governmental and religious resistance. Admitting the certainty of persecution and its strengthening capacity for Christians and churches, Simson sums up the advantage of basic churches as providing persecution-proof environment by saying:

> As God's Spirit resurrects and literally reincarnates the body of Jesus in its organic and original form, and as Jesus, the head of the church, restores apostolic and prophetic patterns to the church, there will be an unprecedented and explosive growth of house churches in many nations. Innumerable people will be saved and incorporated into the churches, the poor and the rich the rural and the urban populations alike. But we should not forget for a moment that, alongside this final harvest movement, what Jesus predicted will come true: persecution will mount like never before, because the devil will realize that now the church really means business. The church is now structured and equipped with the harvesting tool which he dreads the most and which he has spent almost 2000 years trying to obliterate from the planet: the simple, non-religious household of God in the form of house churches.[95]

The advantage then is not that basic churches can escape persecution for believers or for congregations. The advantage is that these methods allow for the constant and unhindered outreach to the unchurched and unsaved. Basic churches provide the most viable methods for reaching people and making disciples in regions beset by manifold trials and persecutions. Christians and Christian groups can follow the methods of starting basic churches with the knowledge that even in areas where persecution may exist, such churches are viable.

Avoiding the Distractions Of Church Buildings

A primary distraction of rapid and uninhibited multiplication of Christian congregations is the provision of church buildings. Church facilities bring problems and distractions that basic churches do not face. The concept that God dwells in certain "holy" buildings led to the creation of church cemeteries where the remains of believers would be safe from monsters and dragons of the deep opened the way to numerous other non-biblical teachings that hindered the outreach of the Christian churches.[96]

Basic churches provide their own meeting places that usually are homes, some public building, or school. These congregations are unencumbered by either providing or maintaining property. The group has unlimited flexibility in the matter of property and meeting places. Many new congregations become burdened and restricted by the buildings that well-intentioned church starters make possible.

Basic churches avoid the problems that permanent and expensive facilities naturally bring. They avoid the burden of upkeep that comes along with church property. They avoid the problem of locality—that is, being tied to a particular community that may drastically change over time. Churches lose all their mobility once they stack one brick on the other. This is not to discredit church buildings but only to surface some of the problems they bring.

Missionaries in Indonesia in 1970 recognized that the method of providing a new church building for every new church would not allow reaching the goal of 1000s of new congregations. The new pattern these missionaries developed called for churches that would meet in houses, be served by lay leaders, and that sought constant multiplication. Indonesian leaders have implemented the new pattern to some extent.

Basic churches avoid the problems of church property. This fact may represent one of the primary advantages of the methodology. These simple churches will not fact the hindrance and limiting nature of church property.

Eliminating the Temptations Of Reliance on Subsidy

One of the more deadening and hindering elements in much missionary strategy revolves around the matter of foreign subsidy for the ministries, a problem often associated with the previous problem of church property. Subsidy places a cap on the possible reproduction of churches in that workers come to think that every church must have a building, equipment, and paid pastoral leadership. Groups can come to the conclusion that we cannot start any more churches than we have funds to support.

Further, subsidy often provides buildings, equipment, and expectations that actually hinder the healthy growth of a new congregation. The buildings provided by subsidy sometimes become a burden to the new congregations and channel resources from the important matters of evangelistic outreach and starting new congregations.

Subsidy often blinds congregations to the opportunities for multiplication and reproduction. These congregations come to think that if they do not have the funds for buildings, equipment, and salaries they cannot start a new church. While subsidy has at times eventuated in strong churches, few of these congregations have been able to reproduce themselves.

Subsidy sometimes hinders the spiritual growth and development of both believers and churches. Since so much of the Christian and church needs are provided through subsidy, local believers (and churches) do not develop spiritual disciplines of Christian living. Subsidy can cut the cocoon too early and leave the developing believers and congregations without strength for living.

Basic church and Church Multiplication Movements avoid many of these dangers. Churches that meet in houses and other facilities the congregation provides avoid the problems of subsidized buildings. Congregations shepherded by lay leaders do not need outside help for salaries and training. House churches, and other expressions of basic churches, do not need expensive equipment. Thus, these strategies escape the traps of many of the dangers related to outside financial support.

Providing Churches that Focus on the Mission

Basic churches and Church Multiplication Movements provide a focus for churches that helps them maintain commitment to the main task. Mandating only the biblical requirements of church also avoids the error of losing focus on the main task. When only the biblical requirements are demanded, the churches can focus on evangelism and Christian maturity rather than any artificial mandates. Facilities, constitutions, vested leaders, patterns of contribution, and mandated actions often eventuate from losing focus on the main task.

In the 1500s, focus on building St. Peter's Basilica eventuated in offering salvation for money in the form of indulgences. When church is simply the biblical church such loss of focus is less likely. Some Christian leaders in England in the 1790s allowed their belief in the doctrine of election to hinder them from accepting the responsibilities of attempting to evangelize the peoples in other lands. Theologically liberal Church leaders in the 1930s lost the concept of missions as calling people to salvation and substituted good deeds and loving service, both good in themselves, for seeking conversion. The effect in all three cases was a loss of focus on the main task and a hindrance to the spread of the gospel.

Basic churches and church multiplication movements help avoid such dangers. By keeping focus on the main task, the basic church movement can be a positive factor in the 21st century. Basic church strategies allow the people of God to concentrate on the main task of evangelism and disciple making.

Allowing Unhindered and Unrestricted Multiplication

Mandating only the biblical requirements of church also avoids the danger of restricting church multiplication. The danger of restricting church multiplication flows from several streams. One, the idea that a new church cannot, or at least should not, start without a sponsoring church or mother church. While the pattern of having a church sponsor the new start is often an effective plan, to restrict church starts to this one pattern can often hinder spontaneous outreach. The *mother church* concept is actually not a biblical teaching but a human invention.

A second danger that can hinder church multiplication is that of demanding trained, often ordained leadership for every new church and limiting church starts by the availability of such leaders. I well remember a meeting of missionaries in Indonesia at which one group insisted we should not start new congregations because we did not have trained leaders for them. As seen, the New Testament does not demand trained, ordained leaders for every congregation that is considered a church. Leadership lies in the harvest. God will raise up leaders for his churches. We must refuse to limit church multiplication to the availability of trained, ordained, and certainly full-time leaders.

A third danger that has been noted earlier that sometimes hinders church multiplication is that of requiring facilities and equipment before a group can be accepted as a church. Some associations of churches receive only congregations that own property as churches. Some groups think a church cannot actually be a church until a building is available. Some groups have limited their church starting to the number of congregations for which they provide, by subsidy, buildings and equipment. These mistaken ideas can lead churches to fail to plant new churches because they do not have the funds for a new church building.

A fourth danger that often hinders the unlimited multiplication of congregations is that of resisting the idea and possibility of Church Multiplication Movements. Some actually resist the idea of such movements. A principle of evangelism and church growth is, "Allow the full possibility of basic churches and Church Multiplication Movements."

No group should contend that basic churches and church multiplication movements are the only methods. Wayner Jacobsen insists that no person view basic churches and Church Starting Movements (not his terms) as the only way and consider traditional churches wrong.[97] These strategies should, however, be accepted and sought. The danger of restricting outreach must be avoided, as a group would seek to avoid a plague.

An advantage of basic churches and church multiplication movements is that of providing safeguards against growth inhibiting factors. Avoiding these dangers holds the promise experiencing the exponential growth the biblical mandate envisions. As health care leaders seek to avoid the dangers of infections, environmental health risks, and physical dangers, the Christian movement must seek to avoid any and all growth inhibiting factors.

Conclusion

Basic church and Church Multiplication Movement methodologies certainly have numerous advantages. These advantages relate directly to the errors and heresies the methods help avoid. Safeguards are closely tied to the methods of basic churches and Church Multiplication Movements. These methods, therefore, should become an integral part of Christian missionary endeavor.

Often what these movements and congregations need most is simple affirmation and acceptance. The Church Multiplication Movement in general does not insist that all Christian missionary effort be channeled into these types of evangelism and church starting. The basic Church Multiplication Movement does, however, ask for acceptance and recognition as acceptable ways to achieve the Great Commission.

CHAPTER 8

WHAT SHALL WE DO?

We have considered the biblical characteristics of churches and Church Multiplication Movements and noted the advantages of such congregations and movements. We now come to the most important of questions, "What shall the Christian movement do in regard to basic churches and Church Multiplication Movements? How should Christian believers, Christian leaders, denominations, churches, and evangelistic groups view and relate to these congregations and movements?

With reference to basic churches and Church Multiplication Movements, Christians, Churches, and Evangelical groups should follow these guidelines:

- *The Christian movement should return to the New Testament pattern of mandating nothing more that the biblical requirements for a fellowship to be called a church.* Human regulations should be set aside. Those fellowships that are composed of true believers, who congregate for the purposes of worship, mutual support, and evangelism, and who follow the pattern of the Triune God should be accepted as churches without consideration for other factors.

- *The Christian movement should accept the fact that congregations growing out of Church Multiplication Movements, out of efforts involving churches that meet in houses, and churches in multi-housing areas have at least as great a chance of becoming congruent with New Testa-*

ment teachings and missional as traditional congregations. Some traditional congregations face the problems of growing large, organizing closely, demanding allegiance, dictating beliefs and practices, and in the end spending most of their resources on themselves. *Mandating only the biblical requirements for "church" avoids many problems, but more importantly, surfaces many of the opportunities of becoming "church" in the fullest and most biblical meaning of the term.*

- *The Christian Movement should encourage and allow these congregations to develop some of their own procedures and methodologies.* Some years ago, I visited a church in the *Kekci* area of Guatemala. A mature man was obviously in charge of the church and the service. He showed people where to sit and suggested when a baby was so loud that the mothers take the child out. But when the message time came, a younger man, who could read, preached. Most traditional groups might find this strange—even unacceptable. But it was working fine in this congregation. Basic churches need the freedom to develop their own procedures that are in line with the needs of their people and adapted to the cultures they serve.

- *The Christian movement should accept and affirm the basic churches and the Church Multiplying Movements as works of the Holy Spirit.* Far from setting up obstacles for these congregations and movements, Christians and Churches should seek to enhance their spread and development. While these movements are the creation of the Holy Spirit and not human endeavor, the Christian movement should study to understand the means the Spirit uses in initiating Church Multiplication Movements. Christian groups should also seek to understand and avoid those actions that prove to inhibit these movements.

- *The Christian movement should declare that basic churches, while fully churches in the biblical sense, do not constitute the* ***one and only pattern*** *for gathered Christian living.* More traditional congregations in various styles will continue to provide evangelism and Christian development through their programs. The basic church movement should not be seen as the substitute for more traditional churches. It is another way not the new way that leaves the old behind.

- *The Christian movement must aid Christians and Christian groups as they seek out new ways for leadership training to enhance the service of the leaders who supply pastoral ministry to these basic churches.* The members of basic churches assume many of the ministry responsibilities that in more traditional settings often fall to the professional staff. Since these congregations expect the members to serve, these congregations must train their members in ways to spread the Message and guide believers. Churches should supply some type of extension, on-the-job equipping for these leaders.

- The Christian movement should seek to understand every culture in terms of segments of the population that may likely respond best in congregations targeted directly to their group. This principle does not mean segregated or racial churches but congregations aimed at evangelizing certain groups. Churches should be established in every population segment.

These congregations should be encouraged to follow the lead of leaders from their own culture and location. The leaders of the basic churches should be introduced to the insights of cultural anthropology so they can adapt their congregations and ministries to the local needs.

- *The Christian Movement should encourage more churches organized along cell-group lines.* In such churches, most evangelism and even discipleship activities happen in the groups. The gathered congregation meets for worship and encouragement. Persons who respond to invitations in the gathered meetings are pointed toward cell-group events. Growth is achieved through the small groups most often led by lay leaders. Sometimes the central church provides overseers for the cell group leaders.
- *The Christian Movement should encourage the development of networks of basic churches for purposes of mutual strengthening and sharing while avoiding any mixture of control or requirements.* Mutual stimulation and opportunity should be sought at the same time that hierarchy and control are avoided.
- *The Christian Movement should affirm and support those works of the Spirit that produce the unlimited multiplication of congregations that remain reproducible and reproducing.* Infinitely reproduci-

> ble and unhindered in constant outreach are imperatives in these churches. Reproducible and reproducing are essential parts of their DNA. By allowing Church Multiplication Movements to flourish around the world (including North America) and by refusing to permit any hindrance to the ministry of these groups the Christian movement will take a valid and needed step in promoting missions in this gospel-needy world.

What then should we do with and about basic churches (simple churches, cell churches, multi-housing churches, house churches)? The answer seems to me to be that we will pray that the Lord raise up multitudes of these small, intimate congregations and used them in an expanding and multiplying nature. We will accept them and recognize them as fully and authentic congregations.

We will support these congregations and further their growth and development. Primarily, we will refuse to place in their path any barriers to realizing the God-given potential and goal of their existence. We will proclaim these congregations and the methods that are related to them as authentic movements of God's Spirit and rejoice at their becoming more and more outposts for kingdom advance.

Further Reading
(Books in Bold Considered Most Helpful)

Robert & Julia Banks, *The Church Comes Home* (Peabody, MS: Hendrickson Publishers, 1998 (second printing 2001).

Robert Banks, *Paul's Idea of Community: The Early House Churches in their Cultural Setting* Rev. ed. (Peabody, MS: Hendrickson Publishers, 1994 [first published in 1979 by Anzea Publishers].

George Barna, *Revolution.* Wheaton, IL: Tyndale Press, 2005.

Dave Browiing, *Deliberate Simplicity: How the Church Does More By Doing Less.* (Grand Rapids: Zondervan, 2009).

Dave Browing, *Deliberate Simplicity: A New Equation for Church Development.* New York: iUniverse, 2006.

Del Birkey, *The House Church: A Model for Renewing the Church* (Scottsdale, PN: Herald Press, 1988,

David Browning, *Deliberate Simplicity.* Grand Rapids: Zondervan Press, 2009.

Neil Cole, *Cultivating a Life for God.* cmaresources.org.

Tony and Felicity Dale, *Simply Church* www. cmaresources, 2005.

Felicity Dale, *Getting Started: A Practical Guide to House Church Planting* (Cmaresources, 2006).

Robert Fitts, *The Church in the House: A Return to Simplicity* (PTWpublish. 2001).

David Garrison, *Church Planting Movements: How God is Redeeming a Lost World.* IMB

Darrell L. Guder, ed. *Missional Church: A Theological Vision for the Sending of the Church in North America* (Grand Rapids: Eerdmans, 1998).

Roger W. Gehring, *House Church and Mission: The Importance of Household Structures in Early Christianity* (Peabody, MS: Hendrickson Publishers, 1998).

Michael Frost and Alan Hirsch, *The Shaping of Things to Come: Innovation and Mission for the 21st-century Church.* (Cmaresources).

Lawrence Khong, *The Apostolic Cell Church: Practical Strategies for Growth and Outreach.* Singapore: Touch Ministries International, 2000.

Larry Kreider, *House Church Networks: A Church for a New Generation (*Ephrata, PA: House to House Publications, 2001).

Nate Krupp, *God's Simple Plan for His Church—and Your Place in It.* Woodburn, OR: Solid Rock Books, 1993.

Robet Lund, *The Way Church Ought to Be: Ninety-five Propositions for a Return to Radical Christianity.*

Milfred Minatrea, *Shaped by God's Heart: The Passion and Practices of Missional Churches (*San Francisco: Jossey-Bass, 2004).

Paul S. Minear, *Images of the Church in the New Testament.* Philadelphia: Westminister, 1960.

Paul S. Minear, *The Obedience of Faith.* London: SCM, 1970.

Reggie McNeil, *The Present Future: Six Tough Questions for the Churc.h*

John Payne, "North American Church Planting Movements," *House2House* Issue 8, 24

J. D. Payne, *Missional House Churches: Reaching Our Communities with the Gospel.* Colorado Springs: Pasternoster, 2007.

Roberts, Bob, *Transformation: How Glocal Churches Transform Lives and the World.* Grand Rapids: Zondervan, 2006.

Wolfgang Simson, *Houses That Change the World.* Emmeisbull, Germany, C & P Publishing, 1999.

Daniel Sanchez, ed., *Church Planting Movements in North America* (Ft. Worth: Church Starting Network, 2006).

Daniel R. Sanchez, Ebbie C. Smith, and Curtis Watke, *Starting Reproducing Congregations: A Guidebook for Copntextual New Church Development* (Ft. Worth: Church Starting Network, 2001).

Ed Stetzer & David Putman, *Breaking the Missional Code: Your Church Can Become a Missionary in Your Community (*Nashville: Broadman & Holman Publishers, 2006).

Elmer L. Towns and Ed Stetzer, *Perimeters of Light: Biblical Boundaries for the Emerging Church* (Chicago: Moody, 2004).

Craig Van Gelder "Missional Challenge: Understanding the Church in North America, in *Missional Church: A Theological Vision for the Sending of the Church in North* America, ed. Darrell L. Guder (Grand Rapids: Eerdmans, 1998).

Craig Van Gelder, *The Essence of the Church: A Community Created by the Spirit* (Grand Rapids: Baker Books, 2000).

Frank Viola, *Pagan Christianity: The Origins of Our Modern Church Practices* (Present Testimony Ministry, 2002).

Rainer, Thom S. and Geiger, Eric. *Simple Church: Returning to God's Process for Making Disciples*. Nashville: Broadman & Holman, 2006.

Frank Viola, *Rethinking the Wineskin: The Practice of the New Testament Church*, .3d ed. (Brandon, FL: Present Testimony Ministry, 2001).

Frank Viola, *Who Is Your Covering: A Fresh Look at Leadership, Authority & Accountability* 3d ed. (Brandon, FL: Present Testimony Ministry, 2001

Frank Viola, *So You Want to Start a House Church: Church Planning for Today (Present Testimony Ministry, 2003).*

James Emery White, *Rethinking the Church: A Challenge to Creative Redesign in an Age of Transition*, Rev. and Expanded (Grand Rapids: Baker Books, 2003) [original publication 1997];

Rad Zdero, *The Global House Church Movement* (William Carey Library, 2004).

Endnotes

---

[1] Daniel R. Sanchez, "Crucial Issues," in *Church Planting Movements in North America*, ed Daniel R. Sanchez (Ft. Worth, TX: Church Starting Network, 2006), 33-58.

[2] J. D. Payne, *Missional House Churches: Reaching Our Communities with the Gospel* (Colorado Springs: Paternoster, 2007), 18.

[3] Frank Viola, *Rethinking the Wineskin: The Practice of the New Testament Church,* .3d ed. (Brandon, FL: Present Testimony Ministry, 2001), 19-20.

[4] Ibid. 20.

[5] Paul Kaak and Joe Boyd, "God is Moving," *House2House*, Issue 8, 5.

[6] John Payne, "North American Church Planting Movements," *House2House* Issue 8, 24.

[7] J. D. Payne, *Missional House Churches,* 8.

[8] Ed Stetzer & David Putman, *Breaking the Missional Code: Your Church can Become a Missionary in Your Community* (Nashville: Boadman & Holman Publishers, 2006), 6-8.

[9] Robert & Julia Banks, *The Church Comes Home* (Peabody, MS: Hendrickson Publishers, 1998), vii, 228-32.

[10] Nate Krupp, *God's Simple Plan for His Church—and Your Place in It.* Woodburn, Or: Solid Rock Books, 1993), 2.

[11] Ibid., 8.

[12] Roger W. Gehring, *House Church and Mission: The Importance of Household Structures in Early Christianity* (Peabody, MS: Hendrickson Publishers, 2004), 26-27.

[13] Wolfgang Simson, *Houses that Change the World* (Emmelsbull, Germany: C & P Publishing, 1999), xiii.

[14] Ibid., 83.

[15] Viola, *Rethinking the Wineskin,* 20-21.

[16] Robert Fitts, *The Church in the House: A Return to Simplicity* (Salem, OR: Preparing the Way Publishers, 2001), 12.

[17] Larry Krieder, *House Church Networks: A Church for a New Generaltion* (Ephrata,PA: House to House Publications, 2001), 57.

[18] Dave Browning, *Deliberate Simplicity* (Grand Rapids: Zondervan Press, 2009), 140-42.

[19] Dave Browing, Deliberate Simplicity: A New Equation for Church Development (New York: iUniverse, Inc. 2006), 133.

[20] Ibid., 134.

[21] George Barna, *Revolutions* (Wheaton, IL: Tyndale Press, 2005), 38-39.

[22] Ibid., iii.

[23]Thom S. Rainer and Eric Geiger, *Simple Church: Returning to God's Process for Making Disciples* (Nashville: Broadman & Holman, 2006), 14.

[24] Ibid., 60.

[25] Donald A. McGavran, "Wrong Strategy: The Real Crisis in Mission," *IRM* (January 1965), 451.

[26] Walter Hurichsen, *Disciples are Made Not Born* ( ), 142.

[27] David Garrison, *Church Planting Movements: How God is Redeeming a Lost World* (Midlotian VA: WIGTake Resourses, 2004, 21.

[28] *Ibid.*, 21-26.

[29] *Ibid.,* 26-28.

[30] John Payne, 24.

[31] See Daniel R. Sanchez, ed., *Church Planting Movements in North America* (Ft. Worth, Texas: Church Starting Network, 2005).

[32] Elmer L Towns and Ed Stetzer, *Perimeters of Light: Biblical Boundaries for the Emerging Church* (Chicago: Moody Publishers, 2004). 69-70.

[33] John Eldridge, "Fellowships of the Heart, *House2House"* Issue 9, August 2005, 7 and 15.

[34] Ralph Winters, *Mission Frontiers*, March April 2005, quoted in House2House, Issue 9, 2005, 8.

[35] Barna, *Revolution,* 16.

[36] Del Birkey, *The House Chruch: A Model for Renewing the Church* (Scottdale, PA: The Herald Press, 1988), 15.

[37] Among many volumes, both older and more recent, are: H. E. Dana, *A Manual of Ecclesiology,* 2d edition with L.M. Sipes (Kansas City, KS: Central Seminary Press, 1944); Paul S. Minear,, *Images of the Church in the New Testament* (Philadelphia: Westminister, 1960); Paul S. Minear, *The Obedience of Faith* (London: SCM, 1970); Jophannes Blauw, *The Missionary Nature of the Church* (Grand Rapids: Eerdmans, 1962); Del Birkey, *The House Church: A Model for Renewing the* Church (Scottdale, Pa: Herald Press); Darrell L. Guder, ed. *Missional Church: A Theological Vision for the Sending of the Church in North America* (Grand Rapids: Eerdmans, 1998); Craig Van Gelder, "Missional Challenge: Understanding the Church in North America,: in *Missional Church: A Theological Vision for the Sending of the Church in North* America, ed. Darrell L. Guder (Grand Rapids: Eerdmans, 1998); James Emery White, *Rethinking the Church: A Challenge to Creative Redesign in an Age of Transition,* Rev. and Expanded (Grand Rapids: Baker Books, 2003 [original publication 1997]; Craig Van Gelder, *The Essence of the Church: A Community Created by the Spirit* (Grand Rapids: Baker Books, 2000).

[38] Milfred Minetrea, *Missional Chruch.*

[39] David Lyons, "Go to the Lost," *House2House* Issue 9, August 2005, 12.

[40] Milfred Minatrea, *Shaped By God's Heart: The Passion and Practices of Missional Churches* (San Francisco, CA: Jossey-Bass, 2004), x, xvi.

[41] Craig Van Gelder, *The Essence of the Church: A Community Created by the Spirit* (Grand Rapids: Baker Books, 2000), 85-86.

[42]*Ibid.,* 110-111.

[43] Gehring, *House Church and Mission,* 46-47.

[44] Robert Banks, *Paul's Idea of Community: The Early House Churches in their Cultural Setting,* rev. ed. (Peabody, MS: Hendrickson Publishers, 1994 (original publishing date 1979), 47-55.

[45] Wolfgang Simson, *Houses that Change the World: The Return of the House Church,* 157.

[46] Ibid., 47-48.

[47]Van Gelder*, The Essence of the Church,* 128.

[48] James Emery White, *Rethinking the Church: A Challenge to Creative Redesign in an Age of Transition,* Rev. and Engl. (Grand Rapids: Baker Books, 2003), 31.

[49] Paul Minear, *The Obedience of Faith* (London: SCM, 1970), 8.

[50] Pheme Perkins, "The Letter to the Ephesians." In *The New Interpreter's Bible*, ed. Leander Keck, 12 vols. (Nashville, TN: Abingdon Press, 2000), XI: 352-53.

[51] H. E. Dana (second edition with L. M. Sipes, *A Manual of Ecclesiology* (Kansas City, MO: Central Seminary Press, 1944), 13-21.

[52] Frank Viola, *Who Is Your Covering? A Fresh Look at Leadership, Authority & Accountability,* 3d ed. (Brandon, Fl: Present Testimony Ministry, 2001), 17-20.

[53] Ebbie C. Smith, *Growing Healthy Churches: New Directions for Church Growth in the 21st Century* (Ft. Worth, Church Starting Network: 2003), 61.

[54] *Ibid.,* 34-35.

[55] Paul Minear, *The Obedience of Faith,* 8.

[56] Among many fine sources see, Roger W. Gehring, *House Church and Mission*, Robert & Julia Banks, *the Church Comes Home,* Robert Banks, *Paul's idea of Community,* Mike Barnett and Daniel Morgan, "Biblical and Historical Foundations for Church Planting Movements" in *Church Planting Movements in North America,* ed. Daniel R. Sanchez.

[57] Roger Gehring, *House Chruch and Mission*, 40-78.

[58] Ibib., 60-68.

[59] Mike Barnett and Dan Morgan, ""Biblical and Historical Foundations for Church Planting Movements" in *Church Planting Movements in North America,* ed. Daniel R. Sanchez (Ft. Worth, TX: Church Starting Network, 2005).

[60] Wolfgang Simon, *Houses that Change the World*, 60-62,

[61] David Garrison, *Chruch Planting Movements: How God is Redeeming a Lost World* (MIdolthian VA: WIGTake Resources, 2004). Garrison's book, which may well be the most important missiological writing since McGavran's *Bridges of God* in 1957 provides many examples of the fruit of strategies involving Church Multiplication Movements and the use of basic or simple churches.

[62] Raymond J. Davis, *Fire on the Mountains: The Story of a Miracle—The Church in Ethiopia* (Grand Rapids: Zondervan Publishing Co., 1966), 109.

[63] Ibid. 109-110.

[64] Charles Bennett, *Tinder In Tabasco: A Study of Chruch Growth in Tropical Mexico.* Grand Rapids: Eerdmans, 1968 (this older book is a valuable source for those concerning with simple churches).

[65] David Garrison, *Church Planting Movements: How God is Redeeming a Lost World,* 36-39.

[66] Victor Choudhrie, "House Chruch: A Biblical Study," *House2House*, Issue 1, 2001.

[67] Garrison, *Church Planting Movements,* 60-64.

[68] Lawrence Khong, *The Apostolic Cell Church:Practical Strategies for Growth and Outreach* (Singapore: Touch Ministries, 2000), 20-21.

[69] Ibid., 35-37.

[70] Ibid., 38-40.

[71] Ibid., 36-37.

[72] Daniel Sanchez, ed., *Church Planting Movements in North America* (Ft. Worth, TX; Church Starting Network, 2006), 530-575.

[73] Ibid,.

[74] Neil Cole, in *Church Planting Movements in North America, ed. Daniel Sanchez* (Ft. Worth, TX: Church Starting Network, 2005), 133-155.

[75] Ibid

[76] Interview of Armando Vera by David Mahfouz, McAllen, Texas, 25, July, 2003. See also, Baptist General Convention of Texas, Borderland Update, Volume 3, Issue 3, November 1, 2002.

[77] Sanchez, *Church Planting Movements in North America*, 33-58.

[78] Browing, Deliberate Simple (2006), x-xxi.,

[79] Payne, House2House, 24.

[80] Viola, *Who Is Your Covering?,* 17 and 121.

[81] For a discussion on this, see Paul G. Schrotenboer, *Roman Catholicism: A Contemporary Evangelical Perspective* (Grand Rapids: Baker Book House, 1988).

[82] Wayne Jacobsen, "Why I Don't Go to Church," *House2House* (Issue 8), 22-23.

[83] John Arnott, "The Supernatural Church is You," *House2House*, (Issue 9), 17.

[84] Robert and Julia Banks, *The Church Comes Home,* 256.

[85] Ibid., 256-57.

[86] Larry Krieder, *House Church Networks: A Church for a New Generation)* Ephrata, PA: House to House Publications, 2001), 71.

[87] Ibid., 228-45.

[88] See Austin Flannery, "The Hierarchical Church," *Vatican II* (NY: Costello Publishing Co. 1975), 369-87

[89] See James McCarty, *The Gospel According to Rome* (Eugene: Harvest House. 1995).

[90] See Simson, *Houses the Change the World* , 61-62.

[91] See Flannery, *Vatican II.*

[92] Browing, Deliberate Simplicity :A New Equation for Church Development, 206.

[93] Simson, *Houses the Change the World, 83.*

[94] Wolfgang Simson, *Houses that Change the World,* 156-66.

[95] Ibid., 177.

[96]Ibid., 69-62.

[97] Wayne Jacobsen, "Why I Don't Go to Church," *House*2House 3.

www.ingramcontent.com/pod-product-compliance
Lightning Source LLC
LaVergne TN
LVHW020644100826
845148LV00012B/2323